The Alzheimer's Cope Book

THE ALZHEIMER'S COPE BOOK

The Complete Care Manual for Patients and Their Families

by R. E. Markin, Ph.D.

A Citadel Press Book
Published by Carol Publishing Group

Dedicated to the memory of my parents, Roe and Lecil Markin, and to the millions of memories currently in peril.

A Citadel Press Book
Published by Carol Publishing Group
Citadel Press is a registered trademark of Carol Communications, Inc.

Editorial Offices: 600 Madison Avenue, New York, N.Y. 10022
Sales & Distribution Offices: 120 Enterprise Avenue, Secaucus, N.J. 07094

In Canada: Canadian Manda Group, P.O. Box 920, Station U, Toronto, Ontario M8Z 5P9

Queries regarding rights and permissions should be addressed to Carol Publishing Group, 600 Madison Avenue, New York, N.Y. 10022

Carol Publishing Group books are available at special discounts for bulk purchases, for sales promotions, fund raising, or educational purposes. Special editions can be created to specifications. For details, contact: Special Sales Department, Carol Publishing Group, 120 Enterprise Avenue, Secaucus, N.J. 07094

Manufactured in the United States of America
10 9 8 7 6 5 4 3 2

Library of Congress Cataloging-in-Publication Data

Markin, R. E.
The Alzheimer's cope book : the complete care manual for
    patients and their families / by R. E. Markin.
    p.   cm.
"A Citadel Press Book."
Includes index.
ISBN 0-8065-1370-5
1. Alzheimer's disease—Patients Care.
        2. Alzheimer's disease—Patients—Home care.
    3. Alzheimer's disease—Patients—Services for—United States.
        I. Title.
        RC523.2.M37   1992
        362.1'98976831—dc20   92-30155
                                                    CIP

Contents

Part 2: In-Home Care

Foreword

Alzheimer's disease (AD), first described early in this century, has become the fourth leading cause of death in America and the leading contributory cause of death among our older citizens. Beyond this, it strips away the most cherished asset most of us have in our later years—our memory.

AD's victims include not only the over two million cases currently diagnosed, but also the wives, husbands, and children of these millions. This book is devoted to those who must shoulder the burden of caring for a loved one afflicted with this disease, in hopes that it will be of some service.

Most books on this topic begin with an in-depth treatise on what Alzheimer's is and its possible causes, and generally use strict medical terminology that keeps laymen either confused or running to their dictionaries. By now you probably know what Alzheimer's is about, so we'll save the strictly medical portion for later and begin with some practical matters that need attention.

As the Director of the Alzheimer's Research Foundation, I am keenly aware of the needs of caregivers for direct and practical information on Alzheimer's Disease. It has been my intention to keep the wording as simple as possible for greater clarity. Likewise, the information presented is in what, I hope, is commonsense order with just the basics put forth. For each major topic addressed there are numerous sources of more detailed information available, some of which appear in the bibliography at the end of the book. It is not my purpose to put forth an encyclopedia, but rather a primer that will serve to acquaint new caregivers with their situation and, hopefully, to help them organize their new lives.

PART 1

Decisions

CHAPTER 1

What Do I Do First?

The doctor has just handed down his diagnosis and, no, you're probably not surprised. After all, you've known *something* was wrong for some time now, right? There have been the signs of memory loss, the depression, confusion, and mood swings, and all the other things that are Alzheimer's disease. So, what's next?

First you must accept the fact that things are not going to be the same. This is harder than it sounds, of course, and the victims' (here I mean both the person afflicted *and* those who care for him or her) reactions run basically the same pattern of emotions as Dr. Elisabeth Kübler-Ross described in her treatise on death and dying: anger, denial, fear, depression, and, finally, acceptance.

Acceptance comes hard. This is especially true in the early stages of AD, when things seem to go on as usual most of the time. Take advantage of this relative calm to get organized. In tactical terms, Alzheimer's disease is not so much a battle as it

3

is a siege, and sieges call for preparation. It is my purpose in writing this book to best prepare you for what's to come.

For now, there are some practical matters that must be handled with dispatch. The order in which the following steps are taken will vary with individual circumstance, but all are important and will be addressed in detail in coming chapters. They are:

(1) Legal actions
(2) Financial considerations
(3) Letters to write, and the family meeting
(4) Home care or nursing home—the decisions
(5) Self-preservation

CHAPTER 2

Legal Actions

Taking Charge

There will come a time when the patient can no longer think rationally enough to be in charge of his own affairs. The time to act against that time is *now*! State statutes vary on what constitutes justification for granting *guardianship,* which is the appointment of a person to manage the rights, property, and/or personal welfare of someone deemed incompetent to act on his own behalf by a court.

Suffice it to say, you don't want to wait until the evidence of incompetence includes severe financial mismanagement or personal misconduct. Cases of AD victims giving away their money and belongings are commonplace, and, as we'll see in the next chapter, now is the time to protect income and assets. Courts are becoming more familiar with AD now, and a corroborated diagnosis from the patient's physician(s) will generally be accepted evidence. Here you must seek the advice of your lawyer.

Finding a Lawyer

There are numerous lawyer referral services located throughout the country, but to locate an attorney who specializes in the type of law you'll need, I would highly recommend contacting the American Association of Retired Persons (AARP). The AARP chapter nearest you can be of immense assistance to you over the coming months, so do contact it early on. Your family lawyer may suffice, and should matters prove outside his or her area of expertise, he or she should know another attorney who can serve your needs.

If you do not have a lawyer who is knowledgeable in the affairs of the elderly or infirm, or a referral service close by, contact the Alzheimer's Association at 800-621-0379 (in Illinois, 800-572-6037). The association (formerly the Alzheimer's Disease and Related Disorders Association) maintains a roster of recommended attorneys, along with hundreds of support groups throughout the United States. I'll be talking more about the Alzheimer's Association throughout the book, but for now you may want to contact it for the support group nearest you and speak with some members of the group, who've been exactly where you are now. Not only can they refer you to an attorney, but they can smooth the road ahead with their experiences.

Guardianship

Guardianship comes in two forms in some states: guardianship of the person and guardianship of the estate. Of the two, guardianship of the estate is easiest to obtain, since complete incompetence need not be shown. Be aware that poor business sense, occasional memory lapses, and physical infirmity are not in and of themselves justification for appointment of a guardian over the estate. Given the rapid decline of mental processes in AD, however, most courts will see the wisdom of granting a guardianship if warranted by medical evidence, recent behavior, or—

and this again you'll need to confirm with your lawyer—the agreement of the patient.

Guardianship of the person requires more. Here it must be proven that the person is incapable of caring for himself in day-to-day life without putting himself or others at risk of harm. Beyond this, there is an element of medical practice known as *informed consent* that comes into play. In a nutshell, informed consent is required for most surgical and many other medical procedures, and without it those procedures cannot be performed. If the patient lacks the mental (or physical) capacity to make these decisions on his own behalf, then a guardian must make them for him.

Powers granted the guardian may be limited or complete, depending on the court's findings of what is required. Here the scope and complexity of the estate and/or the degree of incapacity of the person will be taken into account. If a limited guardianship is granted initially, then another trip to court will be necessary later when the disease has further depleted the patient's abilities.

Powers of Attorney

A simpler instrument that will allow another to care for much of the patient's business affairs is the *power of attorney*. Again, your lawyer will advise here. The power of attorney can be *limited* (sometimes called "special") or *general*. In most states, there will need to be a clause in the power of attorney that states it is to remain in effect after the person granting it (the patient) becomes incapacitated. This is often referred to as a *durable power of attorney*.

Yes, there's another power of attorney you'll need eventually, one for the IRS. Look in the back of your most recent tax return booklet and you'll find a list of forms available from the IRS. It has a special power of attorney form that you must request and have completed to file with the patient's taxes. Some states require a separate form, while others will accept a photocopy of the federal form. A phone call to your nearest tax office should clear up matters for you, or if you use a CPA or lawyer for your taxes you can check with him or her.

Trusts

Another form of granting another control over a person's affairs is the *trust*. If a trust is in effect, there need not be a guardian appointed over the estate. A trust is generally put into place by the affected person, naming an individual or institution who is authorized to conduct certain functions for him in the event of his death or disability. With the proper wording, trusts can last indefinitely.

Wills

Another document you need to have is the patient's *will*. Actually, both patient and spouse need to have wills with codicils included addressing their surviving beneficiaries and the disposition of their estate. There are many financial advantages to having a will, all of which your lawyer can inform you of, and some nasty disadvantages to not having one.

The Alzheimer's patient's competency to execute a will is debated constantly, but in general four elements are required. The person making the will must know the nature and extent of the property to be distributed by his bequeath; he must have a reasonable plan for its distribution; he must know the relationship(s) between himself and those whom he would bequeath to; and he must be able to keep all these elements in mind at the time of execution of the will. Again, your lawyer will advise.

Living Wills

A relative newcomer to the legal arena is the *living will*. This document serves to enforce the patient's right to refuse certain life-sustaining procedures or "heroic" lifesaving attempts. It can only do this if its existence is made known to the health care providers involved, so copies must be given to all facilities where the patient is to receive care. The laws on living wills vary greatly from state to state.

An ethical and extremely personal question arises when we consider the treatment of other life-threatening diseases in an Alzheimer's patient. Do you or don't you? Naturally the patient's input should be the first considered, providing the diagnosis of AD is early enough for him to make an informed decision.

Eventually the patient will lack the mental capacity to make such a decision and it will likely fall to the caregiver. Keeping an already terminally ill patient alive through costly operations and high-tech machinery, only to have him succumb later to Alzheimer's, may seem unnecessarily cruel to all concerned. If so, plan for it! A living will along with proper documentation of the patient's wishes can make this decision easier to make and put into action if and when the time comes.

Other Matters of Importance

Later there will be the matter of civil commitment. It is a fact that AD can effect radical changes in a patient's behavior, and this sometimes goes beyond the control of the caregiver.

We're speaking here of involuntary commitment, and while it may seem a radical course of action, circumstances can warrant it. Since the liberalization of personal rights laws over the past couple of decades, it has become increasingly more difficult to have someone committed to an institution, as is witnessed by the number of mentally incompetents currently sleeping in the streets of our cities.

With so many of these patients now among the homeless, mental hospitals nationwide are reporting up to 40 percent of their beds open. This is something to bear in mind, since should the patient become prone to violence or other antisocial behavior, it may be difficult or even impossible to find a health care facility that will accept him.

Your attorney can advise you about commitment. While we're

on this unpleasant subject, we might as well consider civil and criminal wrongs perpetrated by Alzheimer's victims. Now would be a good time to stop by your local police station and do a couple of things:

(1) Alert the police to the patient's condition. Wandering is a major problem in AD, and it will help if they know to be on the lookout for him or her. It will also help them understand should the patient misbehave in public.

(2) Pick up a missing persons form, take it home, and fill it out. Take this back to the police, along with a current photograph of the AD patient, in case it should be needed later. The time saved in having this done ahead of time could mean the patient's life.

Another place you need to stop is the fire department. Fire departments in some cities provide window stickers that can alert fire and rescue personnel that there is a disabled individual inside. Unfortunately, there have been instances where criminals have taken advantage of this information, so it may be a trade-off of benefit against potential harm. Still, it is a good idea to alert fire and rescue to the patient's condition. Often the first search party formed when an AD patient rambles off is the rescue squad; furthermore, AD patients, because of their forgetfulness, have a tendency to start fires. Emergency personnel can also advise you on ways you can make your home safer.

Criminal wrongs committed while outside the capacity of knowing wrong from right are not punishable by law. This will not keep the AD sufferer from being taken into custody and detained, however, and it is the caregiver's responsibility to use the utmost of his or her ability to prevent such wrongs from happening.

Civil wrongs are another matter. If the AD patient visits a monetarily definable damage upon other people or their property, the patient and/or his estate can be held liable for restitution. This is particularly true in the case of automobile accidents, so removing all possibility of the AD person having access to a vehicle is paramount. If you are on a farm, think of trucks and tractors also.

Before you put this book down and call your attorney, read the next chapter as well. You'll save a lot of time and effort if you do.

Legal Checklist

Police station visit

> Speak with someone in authority about the patient's condition.
> Get a missing-persons form.

Fire department visit

> Alert fire and rescue personnel to the patient's condition.
> Give them your directions to your home.
> Pick up literature, decals, etc.

Alzheimer's Association call

> Ask to be added to its mailing list.
> Find out when meetings are held in your area and where.
> Ask for lawyer referral services.

Lawyer visit

> Discuss your situation.
> Discuss forms of legal guardianship, conservatorship, powers
> of attorney, and wills.

CHAPTER 3

Financial Considerations

Duration of Illness

According to one study, the average Alzheimer's disease patient lives four to eight years after diagnosis. This is not an impeachment of the medical community's efforts, but rather points up the fact that as of this writing, there is no definitive test for Alzheimer's. It is generally diagnosed by excluding all the other potential causes of a patient's symptoms.

At the far end of the scale are those who live twenty years or more after diagnosis. Suffice it to say this will be a protracted illness that will get progressively more expensive, in both emotional and financial terms, as the patient's condition worsens. I'll attempt to deal with the emotional side later, but for now let's consider finances.

Your Balance Sheet

Much of this goes hand-in-hand with what we just covered under legal actions, and, indeed, you'll likely need the advice of your attorney for some items. First off, there's income to consider. Likely, the patient is retired and, if not, he soon will be. If he is still employed, he could be eligible for disability payments through his employer's program. The amount you have coming in will determine what options are available to you and the patient.

Assuming for the moment you'll be caring for the AD patient in your home, there will still be doctors' bills, pharmaceutical bills, some alterations to be made for patient safety and comfort, transportation (if needed), and perhaps some equipment. Ahead will be in-home nursing care, more bills, and, eventually, a nursing home. I do not say this to scare you, merely to alert you to what you need to plan for in the future. To start this plan, write out your assets first.

Include among your assets:

- Income from all sources, provided it will continue after the patient is disabled.
- Equity in real estate. (Here you may want to consult a real estate broker or lawyer.)
- Life insurance policies. (Some policies pay dividends from accumulated premiums paid over the years and some have a loan value. Your agent or broker can help with this, but get your lawyer to check the policies as well.)
- Health insurance policies.
- Burial plans.
- Savings and investments.
- Available government services.

Health Care Insurance

Health care insurance comes in a variety of forms and from many sources. Have someone knowledgeable in the subject go over any policies you might have to see what is actually covered. Some policies will only pay after an exclusionary period, which is to say the patient may have to remain in the hospital for a certain length of time before the insurance kicks in. Often the insurance will pay retroactive to the first day once the stay goes beyond the exclusionary period.

Some insurance will require hospitalization as a prerequisite to paying for care in a convalescent home, and some require this to be a skilled care facility. This is important since most homes in the United States are not rated as skilled care, and many of those that are skilled care are not certified for some government programs such as Medicare. You need to know what your limitations and conditions are before the need arises, and you need to communicate your situation to the attending physician and staff.

In the case of Medicare, all services are provided in full for the first twenty days in a Medicare-certified facility. This is, of course, only available if the patient has been classified as needing medically skilled nursing care. After this first period of twenty days Medicare will then pay a portion of the daily rate for the next eighty days. True, Medicare may pay all or a portion of skilled nursing rendered in the home or in a conventional nursing home, but the prerequisites for this are so strict it is best not to count on Medicare.

Medicaid is another source of assistance, providing the patient's resources are limited. It is a combination of federal and state financial aid that is generally administered at the county level. For the patient to qualify for Medicaid, his assets and income cannot exceed a certain amount. This has often meant the patient must divest himself of assets, or "spend down," to reach the qualification amount in order to receive Medicaid benefits.

It is easy to see what this maneuver would do to the well spouse who must still live within the community. The *Medicare Catastrophic Coverage Act of 1988* contained a "spousal impoverishment" portion that eased that situation a bit. The act established some nationwide guidelines for protecting a well spouse's financial resources when the other spouse requires confinement to a nursing home. It allows the division of assets between the spouses and assures income for the well spouse. Your county social-services department will have all the information you need on this and can assist you.

Many workers are covered by group policies that are handled through their employers. Learn what is in these policies. Dementia may even be excluded specifically as a covered condition/disease. Some may recognize anything beyond age sixty-two or sixty-five as "retirement years" and thus disallow any form of disability payments. In some cases there is a "preexisting condition" clause that states that anything already in progress in the patient at the time the policy is issued will not be covered. Progressive dementia is considered a preexisting condition by many companies and can render the patient uninsurable. There are some companies that prey off situations like this, so don't rush out and buy just any policy that someone will sell you.

Life Insurance

Life insurance is a sore point with me. What began as a straightforward business wherein one paid premiums in return for a set amount to be paid to his beneficiary at the time of his death has become complex. Now there are whole life, universal life, and flexible premium life policies in addition to the simple form, which is term. Too many whistles and bells, promises and provisos. For our purposes we'll consider all forms except term as variants of whole life.

Whole life is the most popular form of life insurance sold today. Popular with the agent because he will be paid five or even ten times as much commission on a whole life sale as on an equal amount of term, and popular with the buyer because that's virtually all his agent ever offers him! In essence, whole life insurance is presented as two things: insurance for a fixed amount and an investment that builds "cash value" over the years. In reality it is either, but not both, and no bargain.

As an example, let's say John Brown has a $50,000 whole life policy that costs him $50 a month in premiums for forty years. At age sixty-five John has amassed nearly $38,000 in cash value in his policy, so he assumes he has access to that money. In a way, he does.

He can *borrow* this money, which should be his anyway, at 6 to 8 percent interest and never pay it back. Really? In truth, he cannot get all $38,000 unless he surrenders his policy, and then he will be without insurance. Whatever amount he borrows, the interest will either be paid monthly in cash or taken from his remaining cash value until it is depleted, and then his policy will lapse. To make matters worse, if he should die while there is an outstanding loan against his cash value, the face value of his life insurance will be reduced by the amount of the loan!

Too many people see their statement and think, "I have a $50,000 death benefit *and* $38,000 in cash value, so when I pass on, my beneficiary will receive both, or $88,000." This is *wrong*. When the policyholder dies, only the death benefit is paid. The insurance company keeps your "cash value." When asked about what happens to the cash value at the death of the policyholder, agents will say something like, "It is included in the death benefit." It is, your $38,000 plus $12,000 of the premiums you've paid over the years for a total of $50,000. You could have had the same amount of term insurance for a fraction of the cost and invested the rest.

What happens is, you are overcharged for your insurance and a small portion of the coverage is placed in an investment account. This "investment" typically pays even less than a bank savings account (4 percent is a standard guaranteed rate, though through the use of "illustrations" the buyer may think he's getting 8 percent or more). A savvy financial adviser, M.B.A., or business lawyer can help interpret these for you to strip away the "legalese" and reveal what you actually have.

In their favor is the fact that whole life policies generally have the same premium for so long as they remain in force. This can prove a bargain once one passes the age where term insurance would be prohibitively expensive, or when changes in medical condition would make the person uninsurable.

Options to Consider

If the Alzheimer's patient is otherwise in fairly good health and can be projected to live beyond a couple of years, it might be advantageous to withdraw that cash value from the insurance policy and place it somewhere where you will get a decent return on your money and it will be yours to keep.

There are single-premium annuities available that will provide an income for either a fixed number of years or for life. Care must be taken when approaching these because of the wording. A joint life annuity, for instance, may pay husband and wife an income, but expire at the death of either and keep your funds! Something with "survivorship" would be better since it guarantees at least a percentage of the income to continue after the death of either principal.

Likewise, there are mutual funds, bond funds, etc. that can provide an ongoing income from a lump sum investment. These vary in return and risk involved and require the advice of an expert.

Equity sitting in a house unused, like the cash value in an insurance policy, does you little good and can keep you from qualifying for assistance. Get a professional to take a look at your financial situation and help you make the best of it. Once you know what you *have,* you can make a better decision as to what your options are.

A relatively new innovation is the *assisted living community.* I feel that as our population continues to age, these will be the wave of the future. In the assisted living situation, you buy or long-term lease housing along with facilities and varying degrees of health care and other services. There may be restrictions on the severity of illness or degree of care required, but as an in-home care option these are worth investigating.

Services Available

It is important to note that some services are available just for the asking. Others require certain qualifications such as age, veteran status, union membership, and so forth. A good place to check on this is with your state/local Agency on Aging. It may not be called that, but each state has something similar. Another ready source of information and assistance is the American Association of Retired Persons (AARP). In addition to a wealth of other services, AARP offers the Medicare/Medicaid Assistance Program, or MMAP. The MMAP is a counseling program for Medicare beneficiaries and their families when they need help understanding Medicare, supplemental insurance, or Medicaid.

MMAP counselors are older adults, generally retired from the work force, who are specially trained in the laws and regulations governing Medicare and other health programs. They give their time voluntarily so there is no charge for their services. If you are homebound you can contact your nearest MMAP counseling service and a representative will arrange to come to you. For help in filing Medicare claims and appeals, verifying qualifications, and assessing long-term care options, MMAP is well worth contacting.

Protecting Your Assets

Okay, now you know what you have to work with. Now let's look to protecting what you have. There have been numerous incidents where AD families have gone quietly bankrupt while a host of alternatives lay well within their reach. Indeed, some services such as Medicaid kick in only after the patient has depleted most of his assets. It doesn't have to be this way.

First, you should move to protect your home. There are ways to do this. Some lending institutions, realizing the situation facing many of our older citizens, have what is known as *reverse amortization loans*. In essence, these mortgages will pay you or at least pay themselves for a time once there is equity enough in your home to guarantee that the loan is more than covered. Check with your mortgage company or banker.

Secondly, you should ask the question, "What is to become of our property when we [or the patient] are gone?" If you are planning on leaving it to relatives, a church, or a foundation, now may be the time to make that move.

If the property is in the ill spouse's name, you may want to transfer it into the well spouse's name alone. In doing so you need not regard the "two-year rule," and you can greatly reduce the ill spouse's assets to assist in qualifying for Medicaid.

You can transfer the title to real estate in most states while retaining a *life interest* in the property for yourself. A life interest guarantees you the right to occupy your home for as long as you live, then reverts to whoever holds the permanent deed upon your death.

The same goes with most property—you can give it away or sell it, yet in many cases retain the right to use it. The subtlety here is to optimize your qualifications for services while protecting what it has taken a lifetime to accumulate. The laws governing such transactions vary widely from state to state, so yet again you'll need the advice of experts.

Now, a word about the ethics of such moves. Many people look at government-provided or -augmented health and social services as a form of welfare and, as such, shy away from using them. Nothing could be further from the truth. Remember, you've paid for these services in advance. Every year you paid social security and income taxes you've poured money into a kitty to be held against the time you'd need help. That time may be at hand.

Your government wasn't shy about collecting your money, remember? And it wasn't embarrassed to spend millions of it on such noble things as experimental hog farms and learning why frogs prefer to mate during a rainstorm, so why should you have to be completely broke to collect what is rightfully yours to begin with? Some open discussion with others in your support group can provide insights into options you can exercise here.

Finally, be leery of anyone who contacts you directly offering something that sounds too good to be true, because it likely is just that. It's a poor statement on today's society but one that must be made; there are unscrupulous people out there who prey on those who can least afford to be taken in. These scoundrels come in the form of salesmen, miracle workers, and, yes, even those claiming to be men of the cloth. Be wary and protect what you have.

Divorce or Separation as an Option

It pains me to think that some of our citizens have had to exercise this radical option in order to secure care for their loved ones. With few exceptions neither of these need be considered today. Medicaid rules now regard the home as an exempt asset and preserve it for the well spouse for so long as she lives. Granted, a legal separation does divide assets among the parties and tend to reduce the ill spouse's holdings. But the law looks more at whose name is on the title when toting up assets, so seek other avenues first.

Protection Around the Home

Another financial matter, though one that may not seem to fit the general theme of this chapter, is protecting your liquid assets on a daily basis. Many are the cases of an AD patient giving away sums of money to total strangers. Some will send every cent they have to a TV evangelist who promises to pray for them, perhaps thinking divine intervention will rid them of the disease. There has even been one case where a sharp, albeit unscrupulous, siding salesman sold an AD patient vinyl siding . . . for a *brick house*!

The shopping channels on cable television can offer some items that will seem very desirable to a demented person who is awake late at night. Later, when the products arrive, the patient may have no recollection of having called for them. If this gets to be a problem, cancel cable or ask for a lock-out box from your cable company. While we're on the subject of late-night TV fare, be wary of those 900 numbers! A demented octogenarian with a rejuvenated libido and a touch-tone phone can add up a huge phone bill. Here your phone company can advise or provide you with service that will exclude 900 lines.

You should separate the patient from his checkbook, credit cards, and any other means of spending—not to be mean, but to protect the patient's (and your) assets. My family learned this when my father, though only in the early stages of AD, developed such a paranoia about money that he actually *buried* $30,000 in cash out in a pasture.

NOTE: Attempting to limit financial access and responsibility in one in the early stages of dementia may be met with resistance or even hostility. It is natural for there to be some reluctance, of course, but there is often a great deal of suspicion. The patient may think his family is in cahoots with his lawyer to rob him blind! Some even go so far as to complain to neighbors or call the police. In general, this hostility runs its course in a few weeks.

In the next chapter I'll cover some letters you'll need to write soon. Your financial situation will determine some of what goes into those letters.

Financial Checklist

Assets and income

What do we have coming in?
Will this income continue once the patient is disabled?
Will insurance and investments provide the surviving spouse
with an adequate income?
How much equity do we have in our home?
Would we be better advised to sell the home and move to
something more economical and invest our equity?
Would it be best to transfer some of our assets to others?

Insurance

What type of disability and health care coverage do we have?
Is there a waiver of premium clause in case of disability?
What is actually covered and for how long?
What is the exclusionary period?
Is prior hospitalization a prerequisite for payments to nursing
homes or in-home care?
What type and amount of life insurance do we have?
Does it have a redeemable "cash value"?
Is there a surrender charge?
Should we cash in the policy and invest the money elsewhere?
If so, where?

Medicare, Medicaid, Veterans Administration benefits, etc.

What services are we qualified for?
How do we go about getting them?
Visit or call your county social services office.

Protecting liquid assets

Collect patient's checkbook and credit cards.

Monitor phone calls and visitors.

Go to your bank and, using your power of attorney, change the checking account so that both your signatures are required if patient is to sign checks.

Monitor phone bill for 900 numbers.

CHAPTER 4

Letters You Should Write, and the Family Meeting

Getting the Word Out

One of the early trials in AD is telling the family and friends about it. Societal impressions are slowly changing for the better, but there's still an element of ignorance where any form of dementia is concerned. What needs to be stressed is that Alzheimer's in its early to middle stages is a transitory thing, that the patient is generally his usual self. Visits should be encouraged, but the visitors should be aware of what is taking place with the patient.

I advise sending letters even if the relative or friend is nearby. Why? Because this is such an emotional issue it is hard to convey your message by voice without the pain and sorrow drowning out what you need to say. In the written word you can be more direct and check to make sure you've covered things as objectively and honestly as possible.

When my father began showing symptoms of dementia I didn't learn of it for some time. Why? Because my mother didn't want us worrying ourselves halfway across the continent and would say everything was just fine, thank you. It is a normal parental instinct to protect the children's feelings, but one that must be suppressed. Knowing the truth early is essential, so tell them.

Family, friends, business associates, fraternal organizations in which the patient was active, church—all need to know of the disease. They need to be aware of what the situation is now and what to expect in the future. You might mention the fact that AD patients sometimes can be unreasonable and even abusive in conversation and actions, then as quickly forget what was said or done. In the case of family members you'll also want to set up a family meeting.

The Family Meeting

At the family meeting you should discuss fully what options are available for the patient's care. Take charge of this gathering and run it as formally as you possibly can. Write out your agenda of items to be covered and do not let discussion wander too far afield! As in any family, there will likely be a diversity of personalities present, but the business at hand is just that.

Do not let any option go undiscussed, though sometimes the mere mention of a nursing home or mental institution will bring abrupt and negative responses. Each family member should be asked what he or she can do to help. Some may be near enough to assist the primary caregiver in the home, to attend to the patient a day or two a week, to do the shopping, to help with cooking or housework. Others may be able to provide financial support. If someone says he can attend the patient a day during the week, ask which day, what hours, and get this time committed on a firm basis.

Obviously it would be best if this meeting is held other than in the home, and definitely not within earshot of the patient! You'll get more honest appraisals, practical suggestions, and realistic commitments if the elements of guilt, sorrow, and even loyalty are held to a minimum.

Warning: Do Not Go It Alone!

There exists among caregivers something called the *martyr syndrome* that must be understood and recognized. In essence, it is the tendency for the caregiver to sacrifice her life to attend the AD patient full-time, all the time. I say *her* because women are the primary caregivers in over 90 percent of all AD cases. *Do not try to go it alone!* Get help and take advantage of it often.

Sure, you'll want to spend as much time as possible with the patient, but realize your limitations. Constant care is a drain both physically and mentally, and you owe it to yourself to stay healthy; you owe it to the patient, too! The patient would surely understand this, if understanding were available to him. Again, you must understand his limitations in reasoning and your own limitations in caring for him.

With this in mind, conduct the family meeting. A suggested agenda would be:

The Patient's Current Condition
The Patient's Projected Condition
The Financial Situation
Care Options
    (a) In Home (and in *whose* home?)
    (b) Care Facilities
    (c) The Costs
Suggestions, Discussion and Decisions

Before we leave this section, there are two other letters I hope you'll write. We at the Alzheimer's Research Foundation are trying to build as broad a data base as possible on Alzheimer's disease and could use your help. We need information on where

AD cases are, age at the time of affliction, vocation, and a host of other variables that will help us target research on this disease and identify potential study populations. In return we will share what you have learned with the Alzheimer's Association and individuals through updated care manuals, newsletters, and articles. Please write the Alzheimer's Research Foundation at the address shown on page 72.

The second letter is to your congressman. It's a fact that there are about 200,000 active cases of AIDS in the United States, and the U.S. government is funding research on this disease to the tune of about $1.5 *billion* this year alone. That works out to be about $7,500 per AIDS patient per year. There are currently over two million diagnosed cases of Alzheimer's disease in the United States, and government-funded research this year is barely $200 *million*, or only $100 per patient!

With up to a million new cases expected this coming year, more emphasis on AD is mandatory. Your congressman needs help in setting priorities, and your letter can be a strong tool. Senator Mark Hatfield recently proposed a marked increase in research funds. His family, like an increasing number of others, has been touched by this disease, and, unlike AIDS research, which has the benefit of virtually the entire entertainment industry behind it, it is up to us alone to let our government know the degree to which Alzheimer's is crippling our society.

CHAPTER 5

Home Care or Nursing Home: The Decision

The Nursing Home

Hopefully you'll read this prior to having your family meeting and do some research into what is available. There is and always has been a negative connotation to the very phrase *nursing home*, and not without some justification. In days when these establishments were not regulated they tended to be dreary and drab, with little or no attempt at providing anything beyond the bare necessities of life. Much reform has taken place since then.

Today there are nursing homes that are filled with light and professionals who are trained in caring for the patients' special needs. Social needs are provided for as well as medical, and some have special programs for AD patients that include speech and memory therapy, reality training, and physical therapy. Not all do, unfortunately, so some investigation is in order.

Nursing establishments are operated by three distinct entities. There are those operated on a for-profit basis by professional groups and corporations; those operated by religious, fraternal, or charitable organizations; and those operated by the state and federal governments. As a rule, the quality and degree of care provided runs in the order listed and the cost in just the opposite.

Nursing homes can be further broken down into three types of facilities based upon the degree of care provided. There are *health-related facilities* for patients who require some degree of nursing and a controlled environment, but who are largely able to care for themselves. There are *skilled nursing facilities*, which provide complete around-the-clock care from licensed and registered medical professionals. And there are *multilevel care facilities*, which are a combination of the two types.

In the typical AD case, a patient would start off at the health-related level of care and digress into needing a skilled nursing facility as the disease runs its course. In a multilevel facility this might mean just switching wings within the same building, which would be preferable to having to adapt to an entirely different environment.

Some considerations to be taken into account when looking at nursing homes in general are:

Its location: Is it handy for visitation? Is it located in a peaceful setting?

The rooms: Are they well-lit and uncluttered? What is the patient load? Is the patient's privacy respected? Are there unpleasant odors? Are there adequate toilet facilities, and are they distinctively marked?

The staff: Is there a physician present at all times, or on call? Is there an adequate number of nurses, aides, and social workers to provide required care and attention to the patients? Are the nurses interacting with the patients, or are they cloistered in offices?

The patients: Do they look happy? Are some smiling, or are they either nodding or staring off? Are they clean and fully dressed? Are they active? Does the staff refer to them by first name, or as *Mr.* and *Mrs.*? (In the case of AD, patients will sometimes respond better to their first names, and this is especially true in female patients who have been married more than once because they tend to regress to their earlier or even their maiden names. *Mr.* or *Mrs.* does, however, imply a certain amount of respect.)

The dining room: How does the food look? Are portions adequate? Do those patients needing assistance eat in the same area as the others?

The activities area: Is there a variety of activities offered, or is everyone just watching television? Who coordinates activities, and how many staff are involved? Are the patients talking with one another?

The philosophy: Is there an ongoing program to keep the patients occupied, or are they allowed to just sit in their rooms? Is there a special program for Alzheimer's patients?

Security: AD patients are known to roam, especially at night. What measures are provided to prevent this?

Cost: How much? Is there a sliding scale according to income? How much, if any, will be covered by insurance, Medicaid/Medicare, or veterans' benefits? What is included in the price? Are some services optional, such as laundry?

I give you this abbreviated list of considerations so you can start to weigh them against homes you may have visited locally. The fact is that nursing homes vary widely in terms of cost. One hundred dollars per day and up is not uncommon among skilled nursing facilities, and $50 per day is common in lesser-care facilities. Not only that, but there may be a waiting list to get in, and this is particularly true in the case of more desirable homes. Then, too, there's the matter of the patient being accepted. Some homes will not take patients who tend to be disruptive or violent, and AD patients can be both. Again, your local social services and your support group can help in locating a facility and placing the patient.

This is a very brief passage on nursing homes, and it is not my intention to give short shrift to something so important. The fact is, there are some excellent guides available at your library and through the Alzheimer's Association and others that can cover the topic in as much detail as you need. You may also want to confer with a caseworker, who will be a far better source locally than any book you can buy. There will be a more detailed chapter and checklist later. For now, we're merely weighing the options.

In-Home Care

The other option is in-home care, and this is the one generally preferred in the early stages of the disease. In a later section I'll address in-home care in some detail, but here we will just consider it in a broad fashion.

The advantages to in-home care are financial, personal, and psychological. It is generally less expensive than institutional care, provided that the caregiver is capable and devoted and that there are not other serious medical factors which will require frequent professional visits.

On a personal basis, keeping the patient at home allows the caregiver constant access and the patient familiar surroundings. Psychologically, the patient draws security from remaining in his own bed in his own home and the caregiver is spared the guilt often associated with the institutionalization of a loved one. The caregiver must bear in mind, however, that there will most likely come a time when in-home care is not the best option.

The decision on whether to place the patient in a nursing home or provide in-home care will necessarily be based on a wide range of factors, most of which we've discussed. The one obvious factor we've not addressed is the patient's preference. Due consideration must be given the patient's feelings on this subject, but as with the financial aspects of AD, his overall welfare and that of others must be placed in the balance, too.

Whichever option is decided upon, there will still be moments when you'll wonder if you've chosen wisely—that is just the nature of the beast. This will be compounded if family members disagree on the patient's care, and there have been cases where hard feelings among the family have been intense. The family meetings, perhaps with a vote, can help allay this and serve to get everyone's feelings on the subject out in the open early on.

CHAPTER 6

Self-preservation

The caregiver is placed in a unique situation. As the AD patient's life begins to disappear from his memory and his physical capabilities wane, it is left to the caregiver to handle these deficits. It is not hard to see that in trying to live two lives the caregiver tends to give up her own. The cost in physical and emotional depletion can be severe if this is allowed to happen. As I mentioned before, you owe it to yourself and the patient to stay healthy.

A Place of Your Own

First, you need a sanctuary. This can be a bedroom, sewing room, den, or whatever, so long as it is exclusively yours. Furnish this room with the things you love, be they antiques, books, music, sewing, or television. Make it bright and cheerful and make it your own; make sure the door has a lock and you have the only key. Now, allocate periods of time during the day when you'll be in your sanctuary and stick to them.

Diversions

Exercise is perhaps the most relaxing and rejuvenating pastime of all. An hour's gardening or walking will keep the juices flowing and give a mental and physical lift to help you carry on. One caregiver I know chooses to chop wood for a half hour each day. He claims that the ability to take out frustrations through splitting logs helps keep him calm and collected.

A hobby can be a wondrous thing. Don't be afraid to try something new. Remember Grandma Moses? Find something that will keep your hands and mind occupied for a while, and have fun at it!

Respite

I've mentioned this before. You'll need it eventually, so start taking it when you can rather than wait until it becomes a necessity. Take some time off, be it a few hours, a day, or a week. Go somewhere, do something, be with other people—and here I don't mean your support group. You'll need to leave everything concerning AD behind and concentrate on yourself.

There will be the temptation to feel guilt at being away but, believe me, you need this. Keep active, do some shopping, visit a park, go to the movies, visit grandchildren—anything you like.

Respite care is available from a range of sources, both for a fee and free. Here your social services director, Agency on Aging, or support group can help. Some cities have adult day care centers, and some hospitals and nursing homes offer daily care or short stays. Do find out what is available and take advantage of it. One recent study showed that *less than 10 percent* of caregivers made use of all the services available to them. Be one of those 10 percent—you'll be glad you did.

Memories

A nice thing to have handy is what I call a memory box. This can be most anything from photos to mementos gathered on trips to objects that remind you of happier times. The patient will likely enjoy these items, too, though there may be frustration at being unable to put a name to a face in a photo or not grasping the significance of some object. For the caregiver, however, it can be a way to remain in touch with the patient as the person he was before AD.

The Present

Stay in touch with the outside world. Read the daily newspaper, write letters to friends and family, make phone calls on a regular basis. The letters in particular are nice because they give you something to look forward to each day when the postman comes.

Something you might consider is getting on the mailing lists for flower and seed catalogs, since the patient would like to get mail, too. The pictures are colorful enough to be enjoyed even in advanced AD once reading skills are lost. Use your imagination.

Some caregivers break their day down into a series of little rewards:

8 A.M.	Coffee and the morning paper
10 A.M.	Sanctuary, reading, or sewing
11 A.M.	Lunch
Noon	Phone friend/relative
2 P.M.	Check mail, walk
4 P.M.	Sanctuary, answer letters
6 P.M.	Dinner
7 P.M.	Hobby
etc.	

Whatever system works for you, use it. Bear in mind that you, too, are a victim of Alzheimer's disease, but unlike the patient you have the faculties to fight it. Don't let yourself become a martyr, and don't let your own life become secondary to that of the patient. Your mental health is every bit as important as his.

PART 2

In-Home Care

CHAPTER 7

Alzheimer's-Proofing

No matter what stage of AD the patient is in when the decision is made for in-home care, there will be some modifications needed for security and comfort. We'll start with security. The idea is to protect the patient from injury in the home *and* protect the home from the patient.

Fire

Limit the patient's access to matches, lighters, and any form of flammable material. One of the early symptoms among AD patients who smoke is having two or more cigarettes going at once, forgetting where they put them, forgetting to put them out, and so forth. Of course, it is preferable for the patient to quit smoking completely, and eventually this will be easier to accomplish. For now, if he must smoke make him depend on you for his light. This hazard is compounded when AD patients are allowed to cook. Not only do they sometimes forget they have something on the stove, but in some cases they confuse the purpose of the oven and tend to use it much as one would a cabinet or even a refrigerator!

Large-handled utensils, using the back burners rather than the front, and having the knobs changed on your stove will help prevent scalds and burns. The potential for disaster here will be greatly reduced if you take measures early, and I'd recommend putting a smoke alarm in each room.

More on the Kitchen

Another facet of the kitchen you need to check is the wealth of potential harm it holds. Cleansers, particularly oven cleansers and drain openers, should be stored in the garage and out of reach. Mixers, blenders, and toasters could all cause serious injury to one in a confused state. Put anything potentially dangerous out of reach.

Knives, scissors, or any sharp-edged or pointed object can be dangerous to you both. Put them up and out of the way. You can get "childproof" cabinet locks at most hardware stores, and they help keep things in their place. Likewise, you need to remember that AD patients tend to put things into their mouths about the same way your two-year-old once did. Small objects should be kept away if your AD patient shows this tendency.

The Bathroom

The bathroom holds almost as many dangers as the kitchen. Medications, hair products, cleansers, and so forth often come in colorful packaging, which makes them look to the AD patient a lot like food. Keep them out of reach and preferably hidden.

While we're in the bathroom, you need to consider the possibility of falls. Remove any small rugs or mats that might slip, and resist any temptation to wax the floors. You may need rails installed to facilitate use of the commode. Also, a grip rail or bench in the tub or shower can help prevent falls.

In-home medical equipment can be expensive, and not all equipment outlets will carry what you need. Some veterans' organizations such as VFW and the American Legion have medical equipment such as walkers, wheelchairs, and hospital beds available for loan or rent at very reasonable prices. Again, your support group will know more of what's available locally.

Around the House in General

Reduce clutter and provide plenty of light, particularly in the bedroom. You'll have less incidents of night incontinency if you provide a clear, well-lit path to the bathroom and mark the door distinctively. You may even consider painting the bathroom door a bright color to reduce confusion, or perhaps put a poster on it that shows clearly what's inside.

Hallways and the patient's room should have night lights. Many types are available at reasonable prices and there is even one with a sensor that will automatically turn itself on and off for about $5, but even though this is not a great expense, you can likely beat this price with a little shopping.

A word on lamps: Bear in mind that the patient will eventually lose some motor control, so make sure lamps are sturdy, heavy, and easy to operate. A push-type switch on the base requires less coordination and fumbling than a switch under the bulb. Also, if you have fluorescent lights, replace bulbs or starters if they make noise or flicker, as this is disorienting and can prompt seizures in some cases.

A final word on lighting. Light is our basic measure of time— it is light during the day and dark at night. With AD there is often confusion over this. Many patients doze off for a few moments after dinner and awake thinking it is morning. To help keep the patient oriented as to time, keep the home brightly lit during the day and reduce the lighting at night.

Wall Adornments

Hanging pictures on hallway walls should be raised or removed to prevent the patient from brushing against them. Hanging mirrors should be removed and stored due to the confusion they can cause to the AD patient who either mistakes his image for someone else at a distance or—and it may come to this—fails to recognize his own image up close.

Sundowner's Syndrome

One of the key symptoms of AD is night wandering, or Sundowner's syndrome. Pacing, insomnia, and reversal of day-night activities are all common. Wandering can be especially dangerous to the patient if he's near a major highway or a body of water, or during cold or inclement weather.

The earlier actions recommended (visiting the police and fire departments, filling out a missing persons form, etc.) can help retrieve a patient who has wandered off. Other measures that can help are a Medic Alert bracelet with the patient's name, address, phone number, and medical condition inscribed upon it, and name-and-address labels sewn into the patient's clothing.

At present we at the Alzheimer's Research Foundation are trying to perfect an affordable alarm system similar to the one used in department stores to prevent shoplifting: a simple alarm stimulus that snaps onto the patient's clothing and sounds an alarm should he go through an exit. In the interim, you can get bells that sound whenever a door is opened and that will help warn you should the patient decide to go roaming. More about this later.

There are currently on the market, and being advertised enthusiastically ("Help! I've fallen and can't get up!"), types of remote summoning devices. While the TV commercials make these seem a logical piece of equipment and service to have, consider this. By the time an AD patient gets far enough along to truly need these things, he may not have any idea how to use them.

On the other hand, some patients tend to abuse these devices (one even used his to tell someone there was no toilet paper!), and there is a charge for each response. The up-front charge for these things may be modest and, when compared to the very life of the patient, which the salesperson will no doubt make, seem completely reasonable. Read on! Some of these devices, coupled with their monitoring service, can run into thousands of dollars. Be certain of the need before buying these systems, and make sure you understand all the charges involved.

Other Safety/Security Considerations

Doors to basements, garages, and any room that might contain hazards should have separate locks to which only you have the keys. You might also try putting a big red STOP sign or even a skull and crossbones on these doors, as some demented persons will associate this with earlier meanings and not proceed through.

Stairs and any rooms the patient will frequent should be well lighted and free of wax, rugs, loose runners, loose handrails, or anything that could cause a fall. Assist the patient up and down stairs and let him know (or think) that you enjoy doing it.

Once more, let me harp on automobile safety. There are several levels and types of memory in operation at any given time, and just because the patient doesn't recall what type of automobile it is doesn't mean he's incapable of driving it. Many's the case of long-time bowlers who, though AD has robbed them of the ability to keep score, can still roll a respectable game! *You* take *all* keys to *all* vehicles (including the riding mower!) and control access to the patient's transportation means. While you're at it, take all the house keys, and be sure to hide a set outside so you can't be locked out.

While we're on transportation, you're going to need to travel to places, and the patient will be traveling with you on occasion. He may not want to get into the car for a trip to the doctor or forget the sequence of physical moves required to enter. You can help with this by "backing" the patient into the backseat while talking calmly. I say *backseat* because that's where the AD patient should ride, and with his seat belt fastened at that. It is not uncommon for AD patients to try to grab the steering wheel, play with the gear shift, or adjust the knobs on the heater or radio constantly. Remember—*the backseat*.

Swimming pools and spas are common these days and pose a particularly deadly threat to anyone with a mental deficit. Keep pool areas fenced in and locked when no one is present. Likewise, the chemicals used in the purification process must be kept secure.

CHAPTER 8

Comfort

The Patient's Room

The patient's room should be light, simply furnished, and easy to maneuver about in. This is particularly true if the patient needs a wheelchair. Before getting a wheelchair, by the way, measure the bathroom doorway—it is often the narrowest door in the house, and you want to make certain the chair will fit through (without scraping the patient's knuckles!).

Furniture should be sturdy and substantial enough to take being ran into or held on to for support. The bed should be low to the floor (even taking the springs and mattress off the frame will help) to prevent injury from sleeping falls. Do not immediately assume you need a hospital bed. There will likely come a time when the patient's lack of mobility may dictate a special bed, but until that time arrives stick with the one he's accustomed to.

A word here about specialized chairs. Remember the precaution about 900 numbers, the shopping channels, and so forth? The same applies here. There are many well-televised products that promise all manner of benefits, such as ease in arising from the chair, motor-driven tilt to enhance circulation, vibrating massage, heat, and so forth.

The immense cost of these things (often hidden in a "low down payment and mere pennies a day!") tends to far outweigh any real benefit they may offer. If your patient needs specialized equipment, let the doctors recommend it and then shop around for the best price.

Decorating Suggestions/Precautions

Plants are cheerful in anyone's room, but there needs to be special care in selecting them in the AD patient's case. Why? Because, as I mentioned earlier, the patient may try to put anything in his mouth. Many common house plants are poisonous! This is particularly true of Christmas plants: Holly berries, mistletoe, and poinsettias are all toxic. Use silk flowers instead or ask your florist or pharmacist which species are toxic. While we're on the subject, right now is the time to look up the numbers for your poisoning hotline and an all-night drugstore. Keep them close to the phone, just in case.

Light colors in the bedroom will make for a more cheerful atmosphere, but be wary of patterned wallpaper, wall hangings, or rugs; they can confuse or even terrify the patient. This is particularly true of wallpaper with animals, plants, or persons depicted on it. Again, be mindful of the fall potential inherent in throw rugs.

Avoid having full-length mirrors on closet or bathroom doors. Likewise, dresser mirrors can startle the patient when he is drowsy or confused by making him think there is another person in the room.

Status/Activity Boards and the Bathroom

Next to the bathroom the patient will use most often, place a small chalkboard. At the top of this you can write in the day of the week, the date of the month, and the year for reality orientation purposes. Also, you can write in the time the patient went to the bathroom and what he did ("#1" or "#2" works well for this). This will help you predict when he may need to use the bathroom and avoid both incontinence and constipation. Simplify this by learning to say directly, "Go to the bathroom!" to the patient, not "*Let's* go to the bathroom," as this sounds like a team effort and can be confusing.

While we're on the subject of the bathroom, alternate facilities may be needed. There are portable and wheelchair toileting aids available that may be helpful, along with bedpans, urinals, and elevated commode seats. Bear in mind that you may need to specify whether the patient is male or female, since there are units for each available in some models.

Also, replacing the locking-type bathroom doorknob is advisable. Not only is the lever type easier to operate, but you don't want the patient locking himself in a room by accident or you out for spite.

Mood

Another soothing touch you can add is music. Music therapy is beginning to come into its own, and this is definitely true in the case of Alzheimer's disease. Monitor the selection carefully, however, because some radio stations tend to switch modes often, and you don't want to subject your loved one to three hours of rap, heavy metal, or even classical music unless that's his preference. A word of caution: A patient's inability to remember the words to songs could be frustrating for him—so choose carefully. Note! New age music is quite soothing. One caregiver plays a tape of a thunderstorm to help her patient sleep and discourage wandering. These tapes are available in the new age section of record stores. (You can also find tapes of ocean sounds, forest sounds, and a waterfall, among others.)

Bear in mind that the things we cherish in health are doubly dear in illness: a favorite chair, our own bed and pillows, a usual place at the table. Care, like love, is a big, serious thing made up of seemingly trivial little things. Take the time to remember these things for your loved one who may not be able to remember.

Environmental Concerns

As we grow older in general, and with AD in particular, we tend to more closely define our comfort range where warmth is concerned. You must monitor the heat/cooling in the patient's room and keep it where he likes it. This, too, can keep down nighttime wandering. A couple of degrees either way can mean the difference between a good night's sleep (for you both!) and a night fraught with restlessness and discomfort.

Radios, stereos, and televisions elsewhere in the house should be kept down lest the patient confuse their voices with those of real people. Likewise, a bang-bang shoot-'em-up movie going on in the next room has frightened many a war veteran AD patient.

Chairs and sofas should be firm; the soft ones are just too hard to get in and out of. Also, watch out for folding chairs and recliners, and chairs that have crossbars between the front legs, which can tangle and trip the patient.

CHAPTER 9

Daily Care

Beginning with getting up in the morning, there will be challenges in caring for the AD patient. Perhaps the first one is bathing and grooming, and this is all-important. For starters, a patient's appearance directly influences his dignity and behavior.

A male patient should be shaved at least every other day, his hair combed and nails trimmed, and generally made to look as neat as possible. Likewise, a female patient needs her hair done, her nails manicured and polished, and makeup applied if preferred. It may be a struggle. You should not *do* these things for the patient, but rather *help* him or her to do them for as long as is possible.

Bathing

Mind the bath water temperature and help the patient in safely. Don't overfill the tub, and do stay nearby. Tub baths are preferable due to the reduced danger of falls. The warm water is soothing and, like a psychological trip back to the womb, tends to calm the patient.

You may even find that the patient will enjoy bath toys again. If so, provide them! There's no harm and the rejuvenation of innocent play is healthy both physically and emotionally. Do assist the patient from the tub and provide a towel.

While the patient is disrobed for the bath is good time to check his or her physical condition. Specifically, check for injuries such as scrapes and bruises or sores. Skin color and general warmth of extremities can give hints as to circulation adequacy, rashes and hives may indicate allergic reactions or irritations. Any radical change should be noted and reported to the attending physician.

Dental Hygiene

Do not disregard dental care, as few things can make life more unpleasant than a permanent foul taste in the mouth or soreness. Dentures must be cleansed properly, fitted with proper adhesive if necessary, and removed before bedtime. A little mouthwash or toothpaste, as the case dictates, is a pleasant start and will help the patient maintain his integrity. "I look good, smell good, and taste good, so I might as well feel good!" is the line of thought here, and it is often the case.

Dressing

Now to get the patient dressed. Again, assist rather than perform for as long as this is practical. You can streamline this process in several ways. First, designate each drawer for a single item, i.e., one drawer just for underwear, one for undershirts, one for socks, etc. Next, *you* control the closet. Turning an AD patient loose in a closet to pick and choose is an invitation to spend a long time deciding, only to come out wearing plaid shorts and a striped shirt . . . in winter!

Limit choice by selecting the clothes beforehand and offering just one item at a time. If you want to give the patient a choice, ask, "This shirt or this shirt?" Not "What would you like to wear?"

Loose-fitting clothing is easier to put on and replacing buttons and zippers with Velcro strips makes it even simpler. Start at the top with the shirt or blouse and work your way down, keeping the patient seated as much as possible. Shoes should fit well and care should be taken that strings are tied to prevent falls.

Feeding

The next challenge is at the breakfast table, a scene repeated throughout the day. Again, limiting choices will facilitate decision making. Many of us, myself included, like to start the day with coffee. There's the danger of spillage and scalds here, which can be lessened by giving the patient a large-handled, easy-to-grip mug that is less than full.

The patient's physical and medical conditions, as well as personal preferences, will dictate what he eats and how much. Just don't be surprised if his tastes change and he refuses something he's loved forever—that is just another symptom, and it may be transitory.

Do not cut up the patient's food in front of him! This, particularly in the early to mid stages, may be taken as a slight and cost the patient some self-esteem. Rather, cut the food into bite-sized or smaller pieces before serving it and—just to be on the safe side—do likewise with your own.

Large-handled utensils are easier to grip and manipulate (these are available as "built-up"–handled utensils from medical care stores; see source of supply listing page 103). and there are antislip place mats available that will help keep down spillage. There may be a mess—try not to react with displeasure or disgust. You will find that a swipe with a napkin can be delivered during conversation and, providing you stick to your original subject, may be accepted without comment.

Picky Appetites, Tastes, and Other Problems

There are some AD patients who make mealtime a real challenge. They make faces at the food, clamp their teeth shut and refuse to eat, or simply do not seem to have an appetite. There are remedies for this.

You can try exercise before meals, a walk, some light aerobics, even dancing, to build up an appetite. Care must be exercised here due to a tendency for the AD patient to fatigue easily. Also you can try serving small portions in several mini-meals rather than just the Big Three. Keep finger foods handy and encourage the picky eater to help himself—many weight-loss specialists will tell you we tend to eat as much out of habit as hunger. Reverse psychology will sometimes work if the patient is playing with your nerves. Just tell him *not* to eat all of something because you're saving it for later. It's worth a try.

Nutrition

Good nutrition is essential, so monitor what the patient actually eats rather than what is served. You can substitute foods as need be or add vitamin supplements to maintain good nutrition. Of particular importance is maintaining fluid intake. Your doctor can advise on how much and whether diuretics like coffee or tea are advisable, but do make certain liquid intake is adequate to prevent dehydration.

The use of gravies and sauces can help the patient to swallow the drier foods and allow a proper mixed diet, but avoid the use of baby food until it is absolutely necessary for the same reason that you never, ever want to refer to incontinence pants as *diapers* in front of the patient. There are many parallels between an AD patient and an infant. Indeed, Alzheimer's disease might well be the "second childhood" folks used to kid about. But you must constantly bear in mind that the patient is *not* a child and may well resent being treated like one.

Communicating

Communication and entertainment go hand in hand. You'll find it easier to be understood if you limit both the number of words in a sentence and their complexity. Think about it. Which is the easier idea to grasp and respond to, "Want to go to John's?" or "Which had you rather do, go to your son John's to play cards or watch a movie, or stay here and make some popcorn?" Listen, you'll hear this type of question asked all the time. It gives too many variables, too many players.

Communication is best at its simplest, and is augmented by a clear voice spoken at a good hearing level along with gestures. Point, shrug, smile, act out what you want done—whatever it takes to make yourself understood. There will still be times when the patient either cannot or will not grasp what you are saying. Be patient and try again.

On the other side, expect frustration and maybe some tears when the patient is struggling to find an elusive word to finish his thought (*anomia*). Don't be too hasty about jumping in to finish it for him, though. Often the AD patient will ramble on with enthusiasm, but his sentences will be a jumble of empty phrases with no point or meaning (*aphasia*). When a meaningful phrase makes it to the surface, reward him for the effort, perhaps with a direct reply and a hug. We never outgrow our love for hugs and, as a nonverbal form of communication, they are without peer.

Try addressing the patient by his first name and using your own name often, too, just to remind him. Communication with those with both Alzheimer's and a hearing deficiency is even more of a challenge. A picture board can help in the middle stages, and these are readily available through your physician or pharmacy.

One of the most dramatic losses an AD patient has to endure is giving up the ability to read. This is particularly true of an individual who has been an avid reader throughout life, and the frustration is intense. If and when this becomes evident, take care to limit written materials in the patient's room and thereby his hurt at not being able to use them. You can still read to him, get books on tape from the library and a host of clubs, and perhaps try the large "coffee-table books," which are mostly photographs.

Entertainment

AD patients are open to a wide range of entertainment in all stages of the disease. There are several very good books on the subject of selecting entertainment for the patient that will virtually guarantee enjoyment. Perhaps the best way to find out what he'd like to do is to ask him. If he says he wants to go chase cars, or women, laugh it off and offer an alternative.

Be mindful that Alzheimer's affects the memory in unique ways. An accountant who can no longer calculate his age may still be a killer checker player. Likewise, an individual (and I've seen this!) who has lost immediate memory to the point he repeatedly asks the same question might do perfectly well in a sophisticated game requiring deeper memory such as Trivial Pursuit. Determine the patient's level and play to it.

For quality-of-life considerations, both yours and the patients, I am tempted to suggest you challenge the patient to the limits of his current abilities. The old adage that what you don't use you lose is responsible for this temptation, but that isn't accurate in this case. Overly simple things will bore or even insult, while operating at the higher edge of capability invites frustration. You just have to try a variety of activities and see what works while realizing that AD is a dynamic thing; what is within reach today may well be gone tomorrow.

Visitors

A word about visitors. By all means, have them over! Just realize some rules are in order. Limit the visitors in the patient's room to one or two. Even two can sometimes be more than the dementia patient can keep up with. I recall visiting my father along with my sister near the end, and his eyes kept switching back and forth between us as if he were watching a tennis match. A single point of focus at a time is easier to deal with.

Secondly, remember that everyone basically loves children. It is, however, a fact that a crying infant in another room may sound like a cat in distress to the AD patient, and three eight-year-olds lumbering around might be mistaken for an earthquake, a brawl, or an all-out frontal assault. Bring the little dears in one at a time; use their names often, along with their relationship to the patient; and let the patient enjoy them at his own pace.

Children, and here I am referring to grandchildren, will need to understand that something is happening to Grandpa or Grandma. How you go about explaining this is, of course, up to you, but be assured they will know. It is best, with any child, to sit him down and speak as frankly as you can. Often children can grasp the situation even more quickly than adults and adjust better. Just be sure their feelings won't be hurt if they're not called by name or there's some confusion as to who they are.

With any visitor, be it a neighbor, lifelong friend, or relative, *do* introduce him by name: "Martha? Our neighbor John Duke is here to visit! Say hello to John." If, as sometimes happens, John starts speaking of Martha as if she were not present, invite him outside and point this out to him. Why this happens is still a mystery to me, but it does.

Do not fall into the trap so many of us do when dealing with small children and the elderly, which is to get cute: "Martha? You want to show John Duke here that fine picture of Abe Lincoln you painted this morning?" She may not be all that enthusiastic to show off her artwork, particularly if her rendition of Abe looks more like Eleanor Roosevelt! You must shield the patient against emotional stress to the best of your ability at all times. She deserves no less.

Medications

The administration of medications in Alzheimer's disease is unlike that of most disorders in that you cannot depend on the
patient. He may forget to take it; he may forget he has already
taken it and try to take it again. He may refuse to take it or want
it all at one time. A Thorazine tablet may look deceptively like
an M&M!

You control the medications by keeping another little chalk
board, marking it dutifully after each dose. It will serve as a
visual reminder to you both. Giving the medication at a fixed
time each day will help establish a pattern with which the patient
can feel comfortable.

While we're on medicines, and I'll likely mention this again,
you MUST be aware of everything the patient is taking. Not only
that, but you must make EACH OF HIS DOCTORS aware of what
medications the patient is taking; an elderly patient may have a
family practitioner, a cardiologist, an internist, a neurologist, a
gerontologist and a psychiatrist all at the same time. Without
knowledge of the other medicines being taken, one of the patient's doctors might unwittingly prescribe something that would
interact adversely with what another doctor has prescribed. Always bring all medicines with you when visiting a doctor or
hospital, or bring along an empty bottle of each.

Toilet

Toilet matters will grow more demanding as the disease progresses. Limiting liquids before bed and encouraging the patient
to go frequently will help limit bed-wetting, but there will likely
be some accidents during even the early stages. The patient soil-
ing himself with feces is more serious, of course, but this is
something that will happen infrequently at first and then as a
matter of course.

There are incontinence pants available that will help with the
cleanup, and lotion-moistened towelettes that will help keep the

patient's skin from becoming tender during the process. Do remember that urine and feces are both hard on the skin, particularly of those who are less mobile, and apply lotions generously after each cleanup.

Also, there is necessarily a high amount of embarrassment that accompanies incontinence in the early to middle stages of the disease. Do not make too big a fuss about it for two reasons: First, it will ease the patient's embarrassment, and second, he may well enjoy the attention and do it more often!

In older men there exists a condition known as benign prostatic hyperplasia, or BPH. This condition occurs in 50-75 percent of men over age sixty. It involves an overgrowth of the cells in the prostate which tends to constrict the opening of the urethra. The patient feels an urgency to urinate frequently, yet may only void a few drops each time due to the constriction. You can imagine the frustration of putting on a fresh incontinency pant only to have the patient go a few drops within minutes. This also interferes with sleep.

You may want to ask your urologist about an operation which can remedy this condition. But, short of that, there does exist a blood pressure medication with the trade name *Hytrin* (Terazosin HCL) which may help or at least delay the need for the operation. This medication is an Alpha blocker which works by blocking the sites on the smooth muscle of the bladder neck and prostate to help reduce the constriction of the urethra. It can be added to most other blood pressure medications in low doses and help alleviate both BPH and hypertension.

Getting Things Done

As AD progresses the simple things become more difficult. The sequencing of events becomes hazy until even minor actions become a challenge. You can help here by arranging sequences in a basic order. To get the patient up from a chair, for instance, place the feet beneath the body to distribute the weight; have the patient lean forward to bring the head over the feet; then have him pull forward with his hands while pushing down on his feet. You may need to assist by tugging gently at a shoulder or pressing forward on the back.

Another oddity of AD is that simple sequences such as just described tend to be forgotten in the conscious mind, yet retained in the subconscious. Patients who can no longer tie their shoes might still be able to play the piano with complete facility. A cabinetmaker who can still cut a perfect joint may not be able to feed himself. The examples are numerous. You may be able to get the patient to do some things that give him problems when being attempted consciously by distracting him with conversation: "So I was thinking that after lunch, we'd go—*sit down here, John*—for a walk."

This comes into play frequently when trying to get the patient into an automobile. There are a number of reasons why this could be true. One patient was convinced that every time he was put into a car it was for the purpose of transporting him to a nursing home, an option he didn't care for at the time.' Another would start to get in by stooping her head, then forget which leg to lift next and get "stuck."

Opening the door and having the patient back into position helps distract him or her, as does conversation while doing it. Just remember to belt the patient in securely and always in the backseat.

Over the course of a day there will be many frustrations to deal with, on both your accounts. Vigorous physical activity has been shown to help dissipate this frustration, so a walk, dancing, light aerobic exercise—anything that gets the heart pumping and lets the mind rest—is highly recommended. This will especially help with our next topic, sleep.

Sleep

As mentioned earlier, patient wandering, pacing, and other activity late at night is a common symptom of Alzheimer's. It can be both an aggravation and a hazard to health. *You* need your rest, and there are few of us who can sleep while a demented person is roaming about the house. On the other hand, the patient needs rest, too, and will be far easier to get along with the next morning if he's slept well the night before.

Physical exercise prior to bed helps reduce this wandering, but may not eliminate it totally. Again, you must not fatigue the patient unduly because, oddly enough, sometimes being too tired will cause insomnia rather than cure it. Having the patient up at a regular hour and replacing naps with activity will help, too. There are drugs to induce sleep, of course, but most have side effects that make this option less desirable than alternatives.

Sleep disorders fall into several categories: getting to sleep is perhaps the most common, so a quick onset of action is desired in any sleep medication; early awakening problems require that the duration of action would closely approximate a normal full night's sleep; nonrestorative sleep, or sleep which fails to adequately rest the patient leaving him groggy the next day is still another problem.

As of this writing *Halcion* (triazolam) is by far the most frequently prescribed hypnotic in the United States. Its onset of action is short, averaging 15-30 minutes, so the patient gets to sleep relatively quickly. Unfortunately, Halcion's duration of action is also short, in the neighborhood of 3-5 hours, so the patient may well awaken in the early morning and pretty much do as he pleases for several hours before the rest of the household is up and about.

There has been much written in the press of late about Halcion, most of it unfavorable. Whether there is merit to these accusations remains to be seen but it stands to reason that someone waking after a mere three hours sleep might be tempted to take another dose, and Halcion like most other benzodiazepine hypnotics is designed for a single dose per night.

Another favorite is *Restoril* (temazepam) which is available in inexpensive generic formulations. Restoril has a longer onset of action, up to an hour, so some preplanning is in order if the patient is to go to sleep shortly after turning in. In its favor is

Restoril's duration of action, which is 6-8 hours. Patients can become tolerant, over a long period of use, which means a progressively stronger dose would be required to achieve the same effect. The main complaint with this drug is the length of onset which pretty much requires one to take it before the need is actually determined. Natural sleep is best, so, if not needed, the hypnotic should stay in the medicine cabinet.

Among the oldest of hypnotics is *Dalmane*. The main problem with this drug is its duration of action which can be as long as eleven hours. Its half-life, or the length of time it takes even half the drug to clear the patient's system, can be over twenty-four hours and there's a risk of building up too great a supply in the blood system if dosed nightly for any length of time. The idea is to help the patient get to sleep quickly, sleep through the night, and awake with as clear a mind as his condition will allow.

A recent addition to the hypnotic market is *ProSom* (estazolam). ProSom offers a rapid onset of action (15-30 minutes), an optimum duration of action (6-8 hours) and is of an intermediate half life so that drug buildup is less likely. According to clinical studies lasting up to twelve weeks, ProSom has not shown any tendency toward tolerance and does not produce the morning deficits associated with other hypnotics. It is available in neatly scored tablets for ease of titration, which is to say you can easily break them in half to achieve whatever dosage the patient needs. It also saves money. In all, ProSom would appear to offer significant advantages over other hypnotics of the same class in the treatment of AD patients.

With all the flap about Halcion in the news, and the banning of it in several European countries and some restrictions on its use in the U.S., many doctors are no longer prescribing any benzodiazepine hypnotics. Instead, some have opted to give their patients medications which produce a desired side effect of drowsiness, such as Benadryl. One must be alert for problems caused by the primary functions of these medications, especially in the elderly who may be more sensitive.

Whichever, if any, hypnotic your physician prescribes, remember to safeguard them well and never use if alcohol has been consumed. If you see problems, discontinue use and contact your physician. If the patient has had a vigorous day with a lot of activity you may want to eliminate that night's dose. It is best if no medicine is used to induce/prolong sleep, of course, but the better informed you are about the options available the better you'll be able to cope with it when the time comes.

Night Wandering

Wandering is a problem, so anticipate it with locks (preferably at the bottom of the door to further limit access) and bells or other suitable warning devices on the doors. Before getting too creative with locking devices, remember the fire hazards mentioned earlier. Check with your fire department about regulations and options available.

Another option might be to provide the patient with a safe area in which to do his pacing. A spare room, perhaps, or a hallway. The same safety principles mentioned earlier apply to this space: Reduce trip hazards, watch what is on the walls, and control access in and out.

Catastrophic Behavior

A final subject that must be considered is what is termed catastrophic behavior. In the simplest terms, these are actions that are abusive, destructive, embarrassing, or even violent. There will likely be some of these, and they range from the baring of genitalia in public to out-and-out assaults. Here are a few examples.

One patient was convinced his wife of over fifty years was selling herself on the streets at night after he'd gone to sleep. Another was certain a neighbor was sneaking into her home and replacing all her valuables with identical yet inferior copies. Yet another felt sure his son (who was fifty years old) was an imposter who'd taken the place of his real son for the sole purpose of stealing his grandfather's shotgun. Accusations flew—along with calls to relatives and even the police—and feelings were hurt.

Another patient decided his sex drive had returned in force, an interesting occurrence given the fact that he was in his eighties and had been castrated years earlier as part of his treatment for prostate cancer. This is a common symptom and one that can cause all sorts of problems. A renewed interest in sex, coupled with diminished inhibitions, can provide the potential for embarrassment if the patient decides to act on his urges. There are several approaches to dealing with this, should it arise.

Perhaps the easiest thing to do is to ignore the suggestions and actions so long as they are conducted in the privacy of the home and no one is threatened. These episodes rarely last more than a few minutes and can usually be waited out.

The opposite action, scolding the patient or threatening him with the taking away of privileges, might work in the earlier stages when there is still a modicum of reason remaining. Be careful not to grant too much attention or you may find the patient will use such behavior to get back at you for imagined wrongs you've done him or for limiting his access to some things.

Perhaps the best way to deal with this is avoidance. During the phase when the patient is actively exhibiting signs of heightened sexuality, limit trips into public places and control visitors. Children in particular must be monitored when they are near the patient. The phase will pass in time.

Sometimes AD patients will say or do things that are outrageous to the point of being frankly hilarious. Here I must admit to witnessing more than a few of these and enjoying them for what they were, momentary releases which, while sad in the greater scope of things, provided some escape from the usual seriousness of the disease.

A case in point occurred before any of us realized my father was beginning to show signs of early dementia. His youngest grandson, aged two and the apple of his eye, came to visit one day along with his mother. As was something of a ritual between them, the child burst through the front door and fairly ran to his grandfather who, as usual, hoisted the child up over his head.

Unfortunately, a wooden ceiling fan had been installed just over their position earlier that day! The child was not injured, though he did sustain several rather audible thumps and spent the rest of that visit avoiding his grandfather. The later scenes of courtship and avoidance kept reminding us of the expressions on both their faces at that moment, and the incident, while sad in origin, was downright funny at the time.

There are sometimes far more serious forms of catastrophic behavior. A patient might reach a point where his frustration or an unfounded fear overwhelms him, causing a violent episode. In such cases you must be prepared to protect yourself first, and the best way of doing this is to remove yourself from the problem. Get away! Failing this, get something between yourself and the patient: a pillow, a sofa cushion, a small table or chair— whatever is handy.

These episodes are generally transitory and a distraction can help bring them to a quick end. One caregiver writes that he always carries the TV remote control with him and, when a violent episode appears imminent, he switches on the television, cranks up the volume, or changes the channel as a distraction. He often turns to MTV, which he recommends as a dandy diversion, then switches to a nature channel that usually has soothing outdoorsy programs.

Summary

This is nowhere close to being a comprehensive home care guide, and I realize that. What I've attempted to do is give a broad brush to the concerns of in-home care along with some high points for consideration, enough to get you started and maybe point you in the right direction. There are several good nursing guides available that go into detail on such items as nutrition, reality orientation, physical therapy, and so forth. Your friends from your support group can suggest these based on their experiences, or you can check with your local library.

PART 3

Help and Where to Find It

CHAPTER 10

Help in Your Neighborhood

As stated before, and I repeat myself here intentionally, there is nothing to be gained by "going it alone." You will need help, and the sooner you admit this the better it will be for both yourself and your patient.

Little things such as going to the store for milk and bread, mowing the lawn, unclogging the sink, and doing laundry take on a more complex nature when one has to include the AD patient in the equation. The good thing is, there are people out there to help with this.

Neighbors and Friends

You should speak with your neighbors as soon as AD is diagnosed, both to let them know what will be happening with the victim and to let them know what your life will be like in the future. If they're worth their salt, they'll be there to help. The same goes for your church or synagogue, fraternal organizations, relatives and friends. Call them.

Your local chapter of the Alzheimer's Association can provide direct help, referrals to available services, phone numbers and names of those you should contact, and, perhaps most importantly, support. Do get in touch with this group and take advantage of this most important asset. Simple suggestions from those who have "been there" are like nuggets of gold. Would you consider the value of soap-on-a-rope, for instance, or would it take a fall to bring it to mind?

Outside Help

There will likely come a time when you'll require in-home assistance. It may be someone to come in once a week to help with housework, laundry, and taking out the garbage, or it may be a live-in nurse or companion. In between there are a host of options. I'll attempt to address each of these in order.

Housework Help: These are generally people who come to your home to clean, cook, or perform other routine, nonnursing chores. They are available from agencies and as independent workers, and some are available through charity organizations, volunteer groups, and churches.

You can find the professionals in the yellow pages of your phone book, in the "Services Offered" or "Positions Wanted" section of your newspaper want ads, and through recommendations of friends. The cost will run from about $5 per hour on up. Always get references, and have a specific list of things you want done since such options as washing windows may cost extra. Most agencies offer bonded employees and this is preferred since, should the employee break or steal something, you would be covered for the loss.

Chore Helpers: These are your basic handymen who do things from simple carpentry to tuning your automobile, fixing flats, installing handrails in the bathroom, mowing the yard, and so forth. The cost is varied, and much of this can be accomplished free with just a phone call to your local Boy Scout troop, veterans' organization, or church.

Visiting Nurses: These come in two forms: from your social services agency and for hire. Most communities have some form of visiting nurse program, and your support group can help put you in touch with one. There is also a Visiting Nurses Association, which is national and may be listed in your yellow pages.

As a rule, the nurse will arrive, check medication and vital signs, assist in moving the patient if needed, and then depart. Longer stays are sometimes available if the patient's condition warrants, but by and large this is a brief visit.

The for-hire nurse costs anywhere from $25 for a perfunctory visit to administer medications, take vitals, and update the patient's chart, to $200 or more a day for an eight-hour shift. IV-qualified nurses fall somewhere in between these prices as a rule. Most of these are registered nurses and capable of rendering the most diverse care of any of the in-home care providers.

Daily Care Nursing: Usually LPNs (licensed practical nurses), CNAs (Certified Nursing Assistants), or MAs (Medical Assistants), these professionals are available through agencies at a range of prices. Those qualified to administer medications, start and monitor IVs, and perform the more skilled of nursing duties will likely cost more. Likewise, the amount of care required by the patient will dictate costs. Items to keep in mind when hiring a daily-care or live-in nurse are: licensing and bonding, compatibility (will the agency replace someone if you, or the patient, and she do not get along?), and the range of services offered.

Companions: This is a broad category that is difficult to quantify. Some can and will take over completely in caring for the patient, allowing the caregiver to return to work or go about a normal social life. Others merely help with meals and take out the garbage. As a rule, a companion will at least help with all facets of care and in running the house, with the cost directly related to the range of services rendered and experience.

Expect to pay from $50 to $100 per day for moderately qualified companions, and even more for LPNs. Sometimes you can find an older, more independent companion who is willing to accept room and board as the bulk of her compensation. These, too, are available through agencies and the newspaper want ads, as well as by referral from friends and your support group.

ALZ-Helpers: If I may, let me address a service that we at the Alzheimer's Research Foundation hope to have available soon. ALZ-Helpers are to be a special group of in-home care providers. They will be specifically trained in caring for AD patients and offered for hire at as reasonable a rate as the market (and our funding) will allow. We plan to augment their salaries with research funds in return for information as well as offering a sort of registry for AD care.

Beyond the usual care rendered, these professionals will perform evaluations of the patient that will be mapped against his or her treatment and medication, with the results going to help increase our knowledge of AD. Interested agencies or individuals who would like to participate in this program should please write us at:

Alzheimer's Research Foundation, Inc.
P.O. Box 9106
Virginia Beach, Va. 23450

Adult Day Care Centers: Once rare, these centers are springing up across the United States and Canada. The cost ranges from free—community, volunteers, and religious groups, and some hospital-operated facilities—to upward of $100 per day. Some offer a sort of "patient-sitting" service by the hour that can be handy and offer the patient a modicum of social life, too. As with any facility, check on licensing, staffing, the physical makeup of the facility itself, and its perspective on AD patients.

Short Stays at Nursing Homes: These, too, are becoming more common and affordable. Many homes require that the patients be ambulatory and in good health and usually state this fact in their ads, but some will take patients in all conditions. Homes are beginning to offer exclusive programs for Alzheimer's patients that include reality orientation, physical therapy, social interaction, and home living retraining.

As a change from a solitary home life, a short stay at a nursing home can be a boon to the patient's morale, and, as a respite for the caregiver, it can be a blessing. As I said earlier, most AD cases eventually require the constant care available only in a nursing facility, and this is a good way to gradually ease the patient (and others in the family) into accepting that day when it comes. Costs and availability vary widely, so check with your local sources.

CHAPTER 11

Choosing a Nursing Home

In an earlier chapter we addressed some of the attributes you should look for in a nursing facility. Here we will expand upon that and offer a simple checklist you can use to help you select one. First, some criteria for determining when it's time to seek a facility.

Necessity

When medical or financial conditions warrant the move, make it. Often the patient will deteriorate well past the point where institutional care is the best option, yet remain in the home due to emotional concerns of the caregiver and/or family members. There is the omnipresent sense of guilt or abandonment that comes with removing the patient from the home that usually doesn't accompany the same action in the case of other diseases and disorders.

You must ask yourself this question, "If my loved one needed constant care for a heart problem, or cancer, wouldn't I be remiss in not providing it?'' Alzheimer's *is* a disease, a wasting one that requires an increasing amount of professional care generally not available in a private home. Realize this and act accordingly. A recent caregiver fought financial hardships as increasingly more qualified nursing personnel had to be brought into her home to care for her father. The arithmetic came down to this: $37.50 per hour for a registered nurse twenty-four hours per day, or $116 a day for a nursing home providing the same care plus a physician, balanced meals, and some social interaction! It took a difference of almost $800 a day—and almost certain financial ruin—to convince this caregiver. Love, care, and duty are hard to place a dollar value upon, but the bottom line is always with us.

Detrimental Effects on the Caregiver

It happens. The fact is, the first line of in-home care is generally the spouse. Given that AD usually strikes those over sixty-five years of age, it is reasonable to assume the caregiver will be in that age group as well. Without taking full advantage of all assets available, and here I mean respite care, support groups, volunteer help, and the whole gamut of assistance there is out there, a lone individual cannot last for long.

Alzheimer's disease, so far as we know at present, is not preventable—physical and mental exhaustion in the caregiver is. At the risk of sounding blunt, there are many stouthearted and loving ladies who have chosen to put themselves into the ground rather than put their husband, brother, or father into a nursing home. Guess where the patient goes when that happens? It's your job to recognize reality, especially in a case where your loved one cannot.

State Hospitals

While not actually nursing homes, state hospitals do offer an alternative in extended care. For years they provided care for mentally ill persons, though often this was viewed as custody as much as care. This was due to the fact that many of the patients housed in state hospitals were there because their behavior was dangerous or disruptive to the point nursing homes would not accept them.

State hospital facilities have been less in demand since the advent of Medicaid in the mid-sixties. Still, there are those who cannot qualify for Supplemental Security Income and, thus, not qualify for Medicaid either for whom the state hospital may be an important option. With certain stipulations, state hospitals can also qualify for payment by Medicare and, if the family cannot meet the financial gap between actual cost and what insurance and other programs will pay, the services will be provided anyway.

Like early nursing homes, state hospitals were not perceived as wholesome places in the past. Today many state hospitals can boost many of the same services as private hospitals. Occupational and physical therapy are available at most along with a complete staff of medical professionals, social workers, and others who genuinely care for their patients. Do visit your state hospitals—you may be pleasantly surprised.

Veterans Administration Hospitals

If the Alzheimer's victim is a veteran you should contact your nearest Veterans Administration Medical Center to inquire about the services available. The VA hospital system contains some of the largest facilities in the United States, and some are affiliated with medical schools that are conducting studies of dementia. There are also special health care centers called GRECCs, or Geriatric Research, Education, and Clinical Centers, which are dedicated to research in the aging processes and attendant diseases.

GRECCs are located at the following VA medical centers:

ARKANSAS	MINNESOTA
Little Rock	Minneapolis
CALIFORNIA	MISSOURI
Los Angeles (Wadsworth)	St. Louis
Palo Alto	NORTH CAROLINA
Sepulveda	Durham
FLORIDA	TEXAS
Gainsville	San Antonio
MASSACHUSETTS	WASHINGTON
Boston (Brockton/West	American Lake
Roxbury)	Seattle
MICHIGAN	
Ann Arbor	

Each of these GRECC centers has a specific area of interest and brings in experts to focus on that particular aspect of aging. Among the areas being addressed are cardiology, diabetes, immunology, neurology, psychiatry, and dementia. You may find a nearby GRECC which offers services that will benefit veterans with dementia, or you may get high-quality referrals to other institutions.

Understand that the VA's first priority is caring for veterans with service-related illnesses and conditions. Due to austere funding in recent years, the VA has been forced to tighten its qualifications for hospital care to the point that besides service-related problems, in-hospital care is limited to those veterans without sufficient funds to get help elsewhere. The formula for computing eligibility is complex, so a VA benefit consultant will need to be contacted. In general, a single veteran cannot have resources totaling more than $22,000 (excluding his home, furniture, and automobile).

Many Americans who graduate from foreign medical schools serve their obligatory first two-year residency in the United States in VA hospitals in preparation for taking the Federal Licensure Examination. This program helps the VA hospitals stay manned with physicians of all disciplines and should be viewed as a plus. The newer medical centers are on a par with the best private hospitals in terms of staffing and available facilities.

Nursing Home Checklist

Visitation

Is the home near enough to family and friends for ease of visitation?

What are the visitation policies?

Are there dining facilities/accommodations for visitors?

Is there adequate parking and/or access by public transportation?

Accommodations

Is there space provided for the patients' possessions?

Is privacy provided in bathrooms and around the beds?

Are exits clearly marked and accessible? Will they accommodate a patient in a wheelchair or using a walker?

Is there a smoke detector in each room?

Are there call buttons in the bathrooms and at each bed?

Are the bathrooms equipped with handrails, elevated commode seats, and sinks and light switches accessible to patients in wheelchairs?

How far to the nearest hospital? Does the institution have a care agreement with it?

Is there a physician present or on call at all times?

Is there a protected outdoor area for patient activities?

Are the heating and cooling systems adequate?

Is the furniture designed for ease of sitting, standing, and maneuvering about?

Security

Is there a separate wing or area for Alzheimer's patients?

Are doors alarmed and other precautions taken to prevent a patient wandering off?

What is the staff-to-patient ratio? Is it adequate?

Is there an evacuation plan posted?

How does the home interact with local police and rescue squads?

Does the home have a file of patient photos and profiles in the event one is missing?

Cleanliness

Does the home have disagreeable odors?

Are the staff members clean and well-groomed?

Do the employees seem enthusiastic about their jobs?

How often is bed linen changed?

How is laundry handled? Is it optional?

Are the windows clean? Do they allow enough light to enter?

Is the paint peeling, and if so, is it lead-based paint?

Do the patients appear clean and well-groomed?

Do the patients seem content? Are they active?

Food

Do the patients have ready access to the cafeteria, or are all meals served in the patients' rooms?

Is there a nutritionist on the staff?

Are special dietary needs provided for?

Does the staff ask for a list of food preferences for each patient?

Does the food appear attractive?

Does it taste good?

Are there snacks provided?

Is the kitchen clean and the dining room ample?

Are AD patients encouraged to feed themselves?

If unable to feed themselves, are AD patients hand-fed in private, or in the dining area with the others?

Are the menus varied and readily available for inspection?

Administration

Is the home certified by Medicare? Medicaid?

Do both the home and the current director have state licenses?

Are all costs spelled out clearly?

Are there extra charges for laundry, hair care, etc.?

Are refunds available for unused services?

What optional services are available?

Will a written statement of the patient's rights be provided to both you and the patient?

Under what circumstances can a patient be discharged, and how much notice must be provided?

Does the institution provide periodic progress reports on the patient's condition and behavior? If so, is this provided to the family, the physician, or both?

Programs

Is there a special program for Alzheimer's patients?

Is there reality orientation?

Is there a daily exercise program?

Is there an ongoing program to train staff on AD symptoms and care?

Are family members invited to participate in treatment planning?

Is reminiscent therapy provided?

Granted, it may be difficult to find a home that will provide every item on this list, but at least you'll know what to ask. More information on homes is available for the asking from a host of sources. Listed below are some addresses and phone numbers of agencies and organizations you will likely need to contact.

Roster of Organizations

Alzheimer's Association, Inc.
70 East Lake Street
Suite 600
Chicago, Ill. 60601
(800) 621-0379 or (in Illinois) (800) 572-6037

Alzheimer's Research Foundation, Inc.
P.O. Box 9106
Virginia Beach, Va. 23450
(804) 427-0220

Children of Aging Parents
2761 Trenton Road
Levittown, Pa. 19056
(215) 547-1070

National Geriatrics Society
212 West Wisconsin Avenue
Third Floor
Milwaukee, Wis. 53203
(414) 272-4130

National Institute on Aging
Information Center
2209 Distribution Circle
Silver Spring, Md. 20892
(301) 496-4000

National Institute on Aging
Information Office
9000 Rockville Pike
Building 31, Room 5C35
National Institutes of Health

Bethesda, Md. 20892
(301) 496-1752

Visiting and Letting Go

Once the patient is successfully placed in a care facility, the next phase, visitation, begins. All those who care for the patient should by all means visit regularly. It is far better to space these visits out among family and friends rather than have everyone show up at once. As the caregiver you should coordinate visitors and ask the home to tell callers to check with you first.

Spreading out visitors accomplishes two things for certain, and possibly a third. First off, it limits the confusion the patient might experience in trying to focus on too many people at one time. Secondly, it spreads the joy of having visitors over several days, which can help the patient adjust to his new surroundings and know he is still loved. Finally, it can force the caregiver into taking some time off.

You should plan your visits in advance. Perhaps you'd like to visit in the morning since, from your experience with the patient in the past, you feel he is at his most alert at this time. Maybe you'd prefer coming at mealtime so you can assist with feeding him or bring him something to eat you know he enjoys. Whatever you decide, you should check with the nursing staff first to avoid conflicts.

There will be some new traumas to cope with here. Likely the patient will ask repeatedly if you're there to take him home. Some will even pack and be ready to go when you arrive if they know in advance you are coming. This can be heart-wrenching. Tears are likely, from you both. Just bear in mind before you get there the reasoning behind the patient being placed in this facility to begin with, and stick by your decision.

Prepare to hear some complaints. AD patients are routinely paranoid and fanciful, so tales of thievery, mistreatment, verbal abuse, and so on are to be expected. Disregarding these stories out of hand could cause a scene if the patient thinks you're calling him a liar, or hurt if he thinks you believe him but just don't care. At the same time, giving too much credence to these things may reinforce their validity in his mind. Just say you'll speak with the staff about it and do, then change the subject.

As this period continues you may find you do not look forward to these visits as much as you did at first. This is normal and part of a process that began much earlier. I am speaking here of letting go. Many are the family members of Alzheimer's victims who have said their loved one's funeral was merely a formality— they'd done their mourning over a period of months and years.

It is reasonable to expect a certain amount of relief when this ordeal is finally over, and equally reasonable to feel pangs of guilt at feeling this way. You will likely experience both; they are the final symptoms of the dread disorder that is Alzheimer's.

There may also be a sense of loss of purpose when the person who depended upon you for everything no longer needs your help. If this is true, stay with your support group; there are plenty of others who do need your help desperately.

PART 4

What's Being Done?
What Can *I* Do?

CHAPTER 12

What's Being Done?

Despite a relative paucity of funding, there is still a lot of research under way on AD. The Alzheimer's Association, through its advocacy program, is helping increase funding for research while at the same time raising funds to encourage other professionals to join the fight. Prominent institutions of higher learning have founded study programs of their own. Still, much is to be done.

Theories

In the simplest possible terms, Alzheimer's disease is a dementing disease or condition of unknown cause. It may be the result of a diminished supply of a neurotransmitter chemical (acetylcholine) that allows brain cells to "converse" with one another, or that may be an effect of the disease.

Here we are playing a version of "which came first, the chicken or the egg?" and all research thus far has proven that a number of anomalies exist in Alzheimer's disease, but which are causes and which results remains the riddle. Until the direct cause is discovered, a cure will likely have to wait. Popular thoughts on the cause of Alzheimer's fall into several camps, though it may well prove to be a combination of these factors.

Heredity

It has been shown that of AD patients who develop the disease at age forty, nearly half their siblings will develop it also. Of AD patients who develop the disease after age sixty, only 20 percent of their siblings will be affected. Likewise, a certain protein has been found on chromosome pair 21 (the same chromosome that carries Down's syndrome) in Alzheimer's patients, yet not everyone carrying this protein develops the disease.

In short, genetics has been shown to be at work in most dementing illnesses. This is not to say genetics is either the problem or the answer. Would that it were that simple! Actually, there are likely several combinations of genes that contribute to the development, or at least the proclivity for developing, Alzheimer's and other forms of dementing illness. The unique combinations of these genes may determine the onset and severity of the illness. Considering that each cell may contain upward of six billion nucleic acids, the possible combinations of these are virtually infinite.

Genetics will likely be shown to "set the stage" for Alzheimer's, while other factors trigger the onset of the illness and perhaps determine its pattern and outcome. A slow-working virus is a favorite culprit for this role among researchers. This is likely the case since genes and viruses interact in many cases.

Again, let me caution against viewing one or even two factors as the whole answer. Each factor should be considered only a fragment of the whole, a contributing agent that, when added to the rest, yields the result. As is often the case with cancer research, each new discovery adds more questions to the puzzle than it answers. Now we'll view some more pieces of the puzzle.

Metallic Invasion of Tissues

Early studies, as well as more recent ones, have shown concentrations of aluminum, bromide, and silicon in the brain tissues of AD patients. There is some speculation that the aluminum compounds used in antiperspirants and in antacids over the past couple of decades are the culprits. As of yet no study has proven this, though toxic pollutants still may prove at least a catalyst to AD.

Before we rush to name aluminum as a contributing factor, consider this. Aluminum is the most common metallic element found in soil. Prior to World War II, there really wasn't much aluminum in use in daily life, yet AD still thrived among our populations. In the less sophisticated societies where aluminum products are still not common, there is virtually the same incidence of Alzheimer's.

In addition, it is very difficult to accurately measure the aluminum and silicon in the brain. Special test tubes of quartz must be used, or enough silicon (glass) and aluminum may leach from the tube itself to contaminate the measurement.

In the past two decades Western societies in particular and the world population as a whole have become increasingly aware of the insecticides and fertilizers used in growing our food and have opted more and more for "organically grown" foods. This may have contributed to the modest increase in some of these elements since the food plant and the animals up the chain are more dependent on what the soil alone has to offer rather than the spray or dust.

The initial discovery that there was an excess (though not a large one) of these elements prompted many questions and observations. Using Dr. Alois Alzheimer's 1909 date of description as "ground zero" and working a decade either side of that, it is easy to see why these observations were made. Prior to 1900 mankind did not drink as much from glass (silicon) and used very little aluminum or bromide.

Since the turn of the century we have taken to these elements in a big way. Disposable aluminum cans are in every home, as are glass bottles, antiperspirants, and antacids containing aluminum *and* bromide in some cases. Is there a correlation? Sure. But there are other factors to consider as well.

At the turn of the century the leading causes of death were dysentery, pneumonia, flu, and a host of diseases and disorders we no longer fear. The average life span fell short of six decades. Perhaps that is the important statistic! Prior to the past generation, people just did not live long enough to develop the cancers, heart disease, and mental problems that are today's threats. Of course, there were not the influences of pollution, food preservatives and additives, and other factors we have today, either.

Slow-Acting Virus

As mentioned, this is a very real possibility and one that is being pursued at several sites around the country and abroad. A virus is an extremely minute organism that consists of genes and a coating of protein—very like a genetic molecule.

In some ways it can be considered as behaving either as a parasite or as a sperm. I say this because of the way a virus acts. The virus will enter a cell by passing its genes through the cell membrane and leaving its protein coat behind. The genes then insinuate themselves among the genes of the host cell and prompt it to produce viral genes and protein, which form new viruses that escape the host cell to infect others.

An important factor in considering viruses is what, if anything, these second and subsequent generations of virus take with them of the host. Do they incorporate host genes into their own makeup that make the invasion of other cells more likely? Possibly. Conversely, the host cell may contribute genes that would make the next generation of viruses less able to cause further problems, thereby lending an antibody effect that would limit the duration and/or severity of the viral infection.

A third possibility is that the virus goes dormant until such a time as a weakness in the host's constitution or other factors cause it to arise and begin replicating again. Examples of this behavior in viruses are the herpes viruses. The herpes virus that causes chicken pox can remain dormant for years before erupting to cause shingles. Likewise, the genital form of herpes (commonly called Herpes II) remains dormant among nerve cells until emotional stress or some other factor brings it to action. The AIDS virus is exhibiting this form of behavior as well.

Research into several diseases that produce dementia similar to Alzheimer's, and are thought to be caused by ''slow'' viruses, is under way around the world. Notable among these is kuru, which is a dementing illness that strikes primarily the children and women of certain tribes in New Guinea. These groups are cannibals and, owing to tradition, the women and children eat the brains of their victims.

On the surface this would seem a purely environmental factor, yet the fact that only half or less of those eating the brains develop kuru would tend to suggest another factor that caused a predilection for contracting the disease. A genetic predisposition is a possibility, perhaps caused by a slow virus that is enmeshed in the genetic tissue and inherited.

Less dramatic in origin, but similar, is Creutzfeldt-Jacob disease. This disease is similar to Alzheimer's, except for its more rapid onset and duration, and has been shown to be caused by an inherited virus.

The difficulty in isolating even one of the larger viruses— along with the fact that most of this must be done postmortem— makes for slow progress in this field. A common factor among the slow viruses is that they cannot be grown successfully in the laboratory. In Chapter 14 there will be a passage on autopsies. Since there is a real likelihood that a slow-working virus is involved, it would be a twofold boon to the research effort if more families allowed the brain tissue of their loved ones who possibly died of Alzheimer's to be used for research.

I say a twofold boon because without this tissue there will be less of the virus to study and without it there can, as yet, be no certain determination that Alzheimer's was indeed present and the cause of death. The world revolves around statistics and, until it is proven that AD is taking an impressive toll among our citizens, it will be difficult to get the amount of attention it deserves.

Hormones and Enzymes

Much new work is being done investigating a protein called A-68, which is found in the spinal fluid of AD patients and may provide a basis for the first definitive clinical test to diagnose Alzheimer's in the living. Since there are numerous forms of dementia that have symptoms similar to AD, it is important that a distinct test be found for early diagnosis.

Current information indicates that a common protein, tau, is altered by an enzyme to form A-68. Questions to be answered are: What enzyme? Why? How? Where does this transformation take place? The answers to these and other questions could yield much in the fight to prevent, arrest, and even cure AD if—and it's a big if—the A-68 protein proves essential to the development of the disease and not merely another by-product.

Most important for our discussion of Alzheimer's is the group of hormones referred to as neurotransmitters. These chemicals enable the various sections of the brain to communicate. This is the essence of memory since recollections are "stored" at various sites in the brain.

There are whole families of neurotransmitters and other hormones to be studied, with new ones being determined all the time. Beyond the production of the neurotransmitters proper are hormones that affect the growth and maintenance of the neurons that produce the neurotransmitters, and hormones that enable the manufacture or conversion of precursor chemicals into the finished product.

It is a long-known fact that the human body undergoes many changes in hormonal activity, and the aging process produces many of these. Menopause is perhaps the most recognized of these changes, but other, more subtle changes occur late in life as well. The endocrine system is definitely a suitable place to search for answers.

The Immune System

There are numerous common areas between Alzheimer's disease and AIDS beyond their seemingly joint rise in public awareness. AIDS always exhibits brain dysfunction and many of the symptoms parallel those of AD. Early stages of AIDS are typified by loss of recent memory, general malaise and depression, difficulty in concentrating, apathy, and a general slowing of the thought process.

AIDS also produces tumors and infections in other organs, but always there is brain involvement and quite often this resembles progressive dementia of the Alzheimer's type. Some medical professionals have begun testing for AIDS in their patients who exhibit symptoms of dementia, and over the past two years over 10 percent of all new cases of AIDS in North America have been in patients over fifty years old.

In the case of AD, there is some evidence that there is a dysfunction in the lymphocytes that control the production of antibodies. Antibodies, proteins that are manufactured by the specialized lymphocytes within the bone marrow and throughout the body, are designed to combat bacteria, viruses, foreign tissue of all types, and damaged tissues. In the case of AD the antibodies may be attacking healthy tissues.

A strong suggestion that this is taking place is the amyloids present at the sites of the senile plaques. Amyloids are commonly found in tissues affected by immune system anomalies, and their presence in the plaques would tend to indicate immune system involvement. Some studies have indicated the presence of anti-brain-tissue antibodies in the bloodstreams of dementia patients. These antibodies are common enough among the aged, but in dementia patients there is an excess that could help explain the progressive deterioration of the brain's function.

It should not go without notice that the brain itself is the ultimate controller of the immune system, and, therefore, there should be no surprise that the two are mutually affected in the case of both Alzheimer's and AIDS. The question at the center of the problem is—as always—why this happens. What is the ultimate causative agent and how can it be defused?

CHAPTER 13

Medications, etc.

THA

New drugs are being tested that, while not really cures, may help slow the progress of the disease. One promising drug is THA (tetrahydroaminoacridine), or Tacrine, which has demonstrated some short-term memory-clarifying results in test patients. These results were not as significant as hoped for in most cases, and the drug has not received favorable reviews by the Food and Drug Administration. The Tacrine study has been discontinued and a royal fuss made about whether or not patients who did receive benefits from the study could continue to use the drug.

THA, as is the case with many other drugs, is not without its side effects and is still under evaluation. The FDA is acting responsibly in its role of protecting the public from unproven and potentially dangerous medications, though it may often sound as though its dragging its feet. One need only recall the thalidomide tragedy of the fifties to realize the wisdom of this approach, but this attitude is of little interest to those whose loved ones are being denied something that, in their cases, helped.

THA will no doubt be looked at again. After numerous other studies it could be shown that THA, in conjunction with other medications and perhaps only among a select number of cases exhibiting certain aspects of the disease, can prove itself beneficial.

We are still in the early phases of research toward a cure. As is the case with cancer, there are what are referred to as "lumpers" and "splitters." The lumpers tend to look at AD as a single disease or condition with one ultimate cause and a single cure. The splitters tend to look at each variance of symptoms as an entirely new disease. The truth is likely somewhere in between and it will take time and money to accurately determine a cause, a control, and a cure.

Physostigmine

This drug prevents the destruction of acetylcholine, the neurotransmitter needed for memory formation. In younger patients the administration of physostigmine has been shown to improve memory function, though not to a spectacular degree. In Alzheimer's patients, however, the results have been minimal.

Part of the problem with physostigmine is that it is so toxic it cannot be given in the quantities necessary to elicit a more pronounced effect. In fact, physostigmine can only be given by injection and even then only acts in the brain for a brief while. A word of caution for those who might consider traveling outside the United States to get physostigmine treatments: The side effects of this drug can be immediately lethal while the benefits are genuinely small and brief at that.

Work is under way to find a drug that acts like physostigmine yet without all its drawbacks. The new drug should be available in oral doses, should last longer, and should be safer. Physostigmine was merely the first of a new group of drugs, and, as with any new invention, it will take time to work out all the flaws.

Choline and Lecithin

It stands to reason that if the body is having problems assimilating choline in the brain, making choline more available should help. Along this line of thought several studies were conducted under placebo-controlled conditions wherein patients were given choline in powder form and lecithin, which is a substance rich in choline.

The results across the test population were disappointing. In general, no benefits were observed, though a few subjects did seem to improve slightly. By the usual rigid standards imposed upon pharmaceuticals, choline and lecithin proved abject failures in the treatment of AD. It is commendable that here the usual standards were relaxed in cases where the patient did improve. Some benefit—albeit small—for even a tiny segment of the overall population is better than nothing at all.

Study on choline enhancement continues. As a commonsense approach it remains in the vanguard of theories on halting the advance of AD. Over a dozen new drugs aimed at increasing the level of acetylcholine in the brain are currently undergoing active testing, all based on the groundwork laid by the choline and lecithin studies.

Hydergine

A popular drug in Europe, Hydergine is a mixture of drugs related to ergot. Its principal action is as a mood elevator. There may actually be an effect on mental function, but current wisdom holds that the elevation of mood, particularly in AD patients exhibiting symptoms of depression, merely enables mental functions to come to the fore beyond the emotional blockage. The mental function in this case could be said to be released rather than enhanced.

Neuropeptides

Peptides are small segments of a protein. They act very much like hormones in that their secretion at one site will affect cells at a distant site. Neuropeptides are secreted by cells in the brain and the ones of prime interest to AD researchers are those that enhance maintenance of nerve tissue. Neuropeptides that affect growth in neurons (the nerve growth factor) actually determine whether these cells live or die.

Other neuropeptides are linked directly to memory and learning. ACTH 4-10, for instance, enhances mental performance in terms of learning and memory. This particular peptide is a segment of the protein hormones vasopressin and adrenocorticotropic hormone (ACTH), and is the only one of dozens of neuropeptides that has been actively tested in humans. Those human subjects, however, were not suffering from AD.

Neuropeptides is an area that will receive further study. The probability that the cure lies in close proximity to the problem dictates this. Since peptides can be said to be genetic material that has evolved over generations, there is always the possibility that one or more of them can be either the cause, the cure, or both.

Surgical Implantation

In the early eighties two patients suffering from Parkinson's disease, a disorder characterized by the loss of another neurotransmitter (dopamine), were not responding to any of the conventional treatments. Borrowing a page from an earlier study wherein elderly rats were infused with fetal rat brain tissue and regained some of their maze-learning abilities, dopamine-producing tissue from their own adrenal glands was implanted deep within their brains. Both subjects showed temporary improvement for several days.

Although the implant surgery yielded but transient benefits in these first cases, the potential for brain tissue transplanting was realized. In Mexico adrenal implant surgery is an ongoing procedure with significant results being reported in Parkinson's patients.

Could it be possible that the implantation of acetylcholine-producing cells from healthy brains into AD patients could yield positive results? Perhaps. The problem here is not merely a medical question but also an ethical one: Where will this healthy tissue come from? There is still much controversy over abortion and the subsequent use of fetal tissues.

Suitable donors other than fetuses would, again, prompt ethical questions. It has been said that the brain may be one organ that will never be transplanted due to the fact that you would be transferring an entire personality into another physical person. The legal ramifications alone—the accountability for past behavior, for instance—are staggering.

Yet it is a possibility within our technological grasp. Hopefully some brave group of souls will attempt this procedure in the near future. As a purely personal matter I don't think I would rest in my grave knowing I'd allowed something for which I have no further use to be buried or burned rather than contribute it to another's benefit.

CHAPTER 14

What Can *I* Do?

What can *you* do? A lot! First, get to know others facing the same problem. Contact your nearest support group and attend the meetings. If you'd like your loved one to receive the latest treatments, get in touch with those who are doing the research. These are usually the teaching hospitals affiliated with medical schools.

Drug Testing

Know what you're getting into before volunteering. The most accurate testing is the "double blind" form. In this type of test there are those who actually receive the drug being tested and a control group who receive a placebo. You are not allowed to know which group you're in, so your actual odds of getting the drug run about fifty-fifty.

As I've mentioned earlier, some of the new drugs have serious side effects, some of which can and do cause death. There are

100

forms to be filled out; there are compliance matters to attend to that may restrict activities, medications, or even certain foods; and the tests may involve extra travel and overnight stays at the hospital. I say this not to discourage you from participating but rather to deal with the topic honestly.

Autopsies

As I mentioned earlier, much of the biochemical and viral research requires brain tissue samples taken after the patient has passed away. Granted, this is an unpleasant thought, but one that must be accepted. Please, to further the chance that we can isolate the cause and get nearer a cure, do allow this tissue to be taken when the time comes.

I look at it in much the same way as I do organ donation: I'm not giving up a little piece of myself to keep someone else alive— that person is giving his all to keep a little piece of *me* alive! Of course, in this case we're not dealing with life. Consider it a final contribution that can help others who could be where you are now. Help make that less likely. Your Alzheimer's Association chapter has an Autopsy Network that can provide all the information, forms, etc. that you require.

And Finally . . .

What else can you do? Write your congressman, your senators, your newspaper. There are millions like you and your loved one out there, and the government needs to know just how many. You might include the phrase, "I'll be monitoring appropriations for Alzheimer's care and research, as well as how you vote." That will get a politician's attention! It is time the fourth-leading cause of death in this country got the attention it deserves!

Take the time to fill out all questionnaires that will be sent to you from government agencies, since every bit of data we can gather will help establish the range and scope of AD in our society. What you have to say is important, your personal observations critical. Many, dare I say *most*, AD patients are seen for a few moments by their physician, given medication, then sent home not to be seen again for weeks or months. Keep a daily journal; write us at ARF with your questions and observances. *You* are the first and best source of information, so please don't keep it to yourself.

And a final plea. Flowers soon fade, just as memories will sometimes do. When the time comes, ask those who would remember your loved one to do so with a contribution to any of the organizations that are working to conquer AD and help the families of its victims. Encourage your church, fraternal, and social groups to support these efforts when they're selecting the recipients of their good works. We all want to be remembered by those close to us, and your help will make that possible—in all ways.

Mail Order Health Care Equipment Suppliers

Abbey Medical

Check your phone book for the nearest office, or call toll free: 800-421-5126 (800-262-1294 in California)

This company offers one of the most complete lines of equipment available, but will only accept orders from health care professionals. Get the catalog and arrange your order through your physician.

American Foundation for the Blind

AFB Products
100 Enterprise Place
Dover, Del. 19901
800-829-0500

This catalog has many items for general patient use along with specialized equipment for the visually impaired. It is available in print, braille, and cassette.

Arthritis Self-Help Products Catalog

Aids for Arthritis, Inc.
3 Little Knoll Court
Medford, N.J. 08055
609-654-6918

A great selection of products for the homes of physically impaired patients.

Cleo, Inc.

Catalog
3957 Mayfield Road
Cleveland, Oh. 44121
800-321-0595 (In Ohio, 216-382-7900)

A wide selection of self-help devices.

Peoples Home Health Care

This is a division of Peoples Drug Stores and may be listed in your phone directory. If not, order the catalog by calling 800-368-4243.

Besides providing a good line of equipment and supplies, Peoples can also assist by providing you with a Certificate of Necessity for all items covered by Medicare. They will also take orders by phone either on credit card or C.O.D.

Fred Sammons, Inc.

Enrichment Programs
P.O. Box 579
Hinsdale, Ill. 60521
800-323-5547

Rivals Abbey Medical as the largest and most comprehensively stocked medical supply source. Unlike Abbey Medical, you can order direct from this catalog without a health care professional as the middle man.

Sears Home Health Care

Your local Sears store can provide you with this catalog and ordering information. Some equipment will likely be in stock at the store.

Bibliography

Alzheimer's Disease and Related Disorders Association, Inc. *Understanding Alzheimer's Disease*. New York: Scribners, 1988.

Bruun, Ruth Dowling, M.D., and Bertel Bruun, M.D. *The Human Body: Your Body and How It Works*. New York: Random House, 1982.

Cohen, Donna, and Carl Eisdorfer. *The Loss of Self*. New York: Norton, 1986.

Danforth, Art. *Living with Alzheimer's Disease: Ruth's Story*. Falls Church, Va.: Prestige Press, 1986.

Frank, Julia. *Alzheimer's Disease: The Silent Epidemic*. Minneapolis: Lerner Publications, 1985.

Gunthrie, Donna. *Grandpa Doesn't Know It's Me*. New York: Human Sciences Press, 1986.

Heston, Leonard L., M.D., and June A. White. *Dementia: A Practical Guide to Alzheimer's Disease and Related Illnesses*. New York: Freeman, 1984 (also an updated edition: *The Vanishing Mind*, 1991).

Mace, Nancy L., and Peter V. Rabins. *The 36-Hour Day: A Family Guide to Caring for Persons with Alzheimer's Disease, Related De-*

menting Illnesses, and Memory Loss in Later Life. Baltimore: Johns Hopkins University Press, 1983.

Panella, John. *Day Care for Dementia*. White Plains, N.Y.: Burke Rehabilitation Center, 1983.

Powell, Lenore S., and Katie Courtice. *Alzheimer's Disease: A Guide for Families*. Reading, Mass.: Addison-Wesley, 1983.

Reisberg, Barry, M.D. *A Guide to Alzheimer's Disease: For Families, Spouses and Friends*. New York: Free Press, 1983.

Roach, Marion. *Another Name for Madness*. Boston: Houghton Mifflin, 1985.

Scully, Thomas, M.D., and Cynthia Scully. *Playing God: The New World of Medical Choices*. New York: Simon and Schuster, 1988.

Sheridan, Carmel. *Failure-Free Activities for the Alzheimer's Patient: A Guidebook for Caregivers*. Lake Bluff, Ill.: Quality Books, 1988.

U.S. Congress, Office of Technology. *Losing a Million Minds*. Washington, D.C.: Government Printing Office, 1987.

Zarit, Steven H., Nancy K. Orr, and Judy M. Zarit. *The Hidden Victims of Alzheimer's Disease: Families Under Stress*. New York: University Press, 1985.

Index